PRAISE FOR
WITH LOVE FROM A CHILDREN'S THERAPIST

"Powerful. Heartfelt. Eye-opening. Stacy takes readers on a profound journey through trauma and healing, bravely sharing her own pain-filled story alongside the stories of her clients. With the wisdom of a seasoned therapist, she weaves together insights and reflections that not only deepen our understanding of trauma but also illuminate the resilience and empowerment that emerge from it. She fearlessly addresses the topics we often shy away from, bringing them into the light with compassion and clarity. This book will touch your heart, bring tears to your eyes, and offer a raw, lived experience of trauma—far beyond the pages of a textbook."
—**Lisa Dion, LPC, RPT-S**, president of Synergetic Play Therapy Institute, creator of Synergetic Play Therapy

"In *With Love from a Children's Therapist*, Stacy Schaffer writes from the heart for the heart. In her book, Schaffer describes story after story of the power of earned security, which is an attachment concept to describe how finding healing after trauma can occur when we find our 'birthday candles'—with those who provide a sense of safety and trust in our lives, which take place in relationships throughout our lives. Schaffer interweaves stories of her own healing while discussing difficult topics and concepts, and does so in an approachable, easy-to-understand manner. Her love for her clinical work shines through as does her humor and knowledge."
—**Clair Mellenthin, PhD, RPT-S**, creator of Attachment Centered Play Therapy

"In a powerful and poignant blend of telling her own story and the stories of kids in her office, Stacy Schaffer illuminates important truths about vulnerability, healing, and resilience for all ages. Hitting directly on real things that kids and grown-ups struggle with, *With Love from a Children's Therapist* will help parents feel more resourced in supporting their kids, it will help individuals of all ages own and honor their stories in meaningful ways, and it will help all of us open up to the power of healing, honesty, and community in our fragmented world."

—**Kathy Escobar**, cofounder of The Refuge and author of *Practicing: Changing Yourself to Change the World*

"More important than education is lived experience. When you have both—guiding you through a book or a therapy session—you have *With Love from a Children's Therapist*. Stacy uses her personal narrative to highlight the trials and triumphs so many of us face. This book is a combination of professional insight and profound wisdom and will enlighten every parent or provider who finds themselves within the pages."

—**Stephanie Hanrahan**, author, autism activist, and founder of the viral online community Tinkles Her Pants

"I have had the pleasure of knowing and working alongside Ms. Schaffer for over ten years, and I can confidently say that she is an exceptional mental health specialist. Using her own life experiences, Ms. Schaffer has a unique ability to relate to and form meaningful connections with her young patients. Her insight and empathy allow her to truly understand their challenges, enabling her to provide tailored support that addresses their specific needs. The blend of her personal experiences and professional expertise clearly sets her apart, making her a highly trusted and recommended therapist. Her

book, *With Love from a Children's Therapist*, offers valuable insight into pediatric mental health as well. I highly recommend her book."
—**Veena Mathad, MD**, pediatrician, owner of Sunflower Pediatrics

"In the midst of a youth mental health crisis in the US, Stacy offers a rare and powerful window into the hopes, struggles, dreams, and realities of today's young people. With empathy, humor, and a deeply personal reflection on her own life, she challenges us to meet the expectations that young people have of the adults around them. Her insights are a gift to anyone seeking to break generational cycles and raise resilient, confident children in a world that often seems ill-equipped to support childhood."
—**Carolyn McDonald, LCSW, PMH-C**

"Stacy is a beacon of light in the lives of the clients she serves and the community she has cultivated. She has an innate gift in being able to name the sorrow and beauty inherent in our work with clients as well as the societal backdrop that influences these relationships. Most of all, she speaks and writes with a kind of gentle amusement that allows us to hold difficulties with a sense of levity, extending permission to take ourselves just a little less seriously."
—**Kayla Bettis-Weber, LCSW, LAC, ACS**

"Stacy Schaffer has woven a mesmerizing story with insights and musings from her tumultuous childhood, her career as a children's therapist, and her tight-knit community. She has successfully written a funny, witty, and achingly raw portrayal of what it is like to treat children facing an array of life challenges. This book is a must read for anyone who cares for

children or was once a child navigating this wild and scary life. A brilliant book from start to finish. It will make you want to get your own Stacy."
—**Nikki Kennedy, LPC**, therapist, friend, teacher, mother

"Stacy has developed well-earned wisdom from the chaos and trauma she endured. While much of her story could've turned her down a dark path—she has chosen an authentic purple path of light and love. As both a colleague and friend, I relish her insight and humor, which will keep you turning the pages."
—**Maia Longenecker, LCSW**, executive director of Blue Channel Therapy

"Stacy Schaffer has written a powerful and insightful offering that weaves together the wisdom gained from her years of clinical experience as a child and youth therapist alongside the story of her own harrowing and devastating childhood trauma. With forthright honesty and cutting wit, this book presents an inside look at some of the challenges today's youth face while living in an unpredictable, overwhelming, and sometimes unsafe world. Stacy has taken her own traumatic experiences and courageously transformed her pain into a lifelong commitment to helping others feel seen, heard, and witnessed. *With Love from a Children's Therapist* is a deeply empathetic, inspiring, and engaging plea to all people who love children and youth to wake up and recognize the unique and sometimes impossible challenges they are facing and how we can all take steps to be a safe, supportive, and healing presence."
—**Khristine Turner Rolfe, LCMHC, RPT-S**, child therapist and supervisor

WITH LOVE
FROM A
CHILDREN'S THERAPIST

#lessonsihavelearnedalongtheway

STACY SCHAFFER, MA, LPC

MEDIA.COM

With Love from a Children's Therapist
Copyright © 2025 by Stacy Schaffer, MA, LPC

All rights reserved. No part of this book may be reproduced in any form or by any means—whether electronic, digital, mechanical, or otherwise—without permission in writing from the publisher, except by a reviewer, who may quote brief passages in a review.

The views and opinions expressed in this book are those of the author and do not necessarily reflect the official policy or position of Illumify Media Global.

To protect the privacy of the author's clients, names and identifying details have been altered.

Published by
Illumify Media Global
www.IllumifyMedia.com
"Let's bring your book to life!"

Paperback ISBN: 978-1-964251-51-6
Hardcover ISBN: 978-1-964251-62-2

Cover design by Debbie Lewis

Printed in the United States of America

For my brave and brilliant clients, past, present, and future. Thank you for trusting me with the deepest layers of your heart, sharing your innate wisdom, and revealing the most challenging parts of your journeys. I am absolutely a healthier human because of learning how to better support the healing of the younger generations. This book is dedicated to all of you.

CONTENTS

Acknowledgments xi
Introduction xv

1	#silentnomore: *Trauma Recovery*	1
2	#olafwithaz: *Anxiety Enters the Chat*	7
3	#denyingthedragon: *The Reality of Suicidality*	16
4	#needymcneedersonpants: *Needs Welcomed Here*	26
5	#truthbombs: *Bite-Sized Snippets*	33
6	#barbiewasntwrong: *Equality Messages Matter*	43
7	#retreatingwithin: *Dissociation Is a Trip*	51
8	#waitforit: *Control Issues*	60
9	#empathytraining: *How to Help*	68
10	#andalso: *Holding Concurrent Realities*	81
11	#strongheartsclub: *The Grief Pilgrimage*	90
12	#plottwist: *Changing the Narrative*	107
13	#getyourownstacy: *Doing Your Inner Work*	119
14	#hellodarknessmyoldfriend: *Depression Is a Repeat Offender*	130
15	#teeth: *Family Values*	142
16	#fromtheotherside: *What Kids Wish Grown-ups Knew*	154
17	#lastvegasnerve: *Ultra-Neon Dysregulation*	164
18	#notmymothersbody: *Body-Shaming Culture Vibes*	174
19	#preapproved: *Approval Addiction*	183
20	#hoperestored: *Because Redemption*	197

Appendix   #withlove: *Closing Thoughts* 202
Notes 206

ACKNOWLEDGMENTS

WHEN PEOPLE HEAR THE REALITY I have no actual living family, the first response is a concerned combination of tilted head pity and wide-eyed curiosity. There is no need for that. Support? Please. Trust me, there are so many phenomenal people to thank and not enough time. Honorary family surrounds me, and I am completely overflowing with gratitude. Seriously.

While there are so many individual people to thank in my life in general, there were a select few who definitely made this book dream become possible. If it weren't for incredible cheerleaders in my life, this project would have never come to fruition. Like ever.

I would like to send out special thanks to those who, without their support, *With Love* would not have transformed into what it has become.

Kathy Escobar, for being my honorary mom, teammate, head cheerleader, and friend, all wrapped in one. Her belief in me, for approaching two decades now, has structurally shifted who I am as a person—and therefore the author I became.

Sherrey Neckers, for her phenomenal ability to know exactly how to show up, how to see through to the beauty when it feels lost, and for always being a safe place to land. Thank you for letting me not give up on myself and instead always offering a real lifeline at a moment's notice.

Katie Peterson, for her commitment to making sure both deep rest and special celebrations take place for me. You are one of the best parts about being alive.

Melissa Romano, for her relentless intensity for my healing and for being the safest place possible to process the content within these pages. Thank you for deeply understanding me. Melissa, you are really stuck with me now.

Jordan White, for his encouragement to begin this project in the first place. Thank you for challenging me to conquer the fear that stood in my way and for always being in my corner.

Carolyn McDonald, for her consistent support, chapter by chapter, each step of the way. Her championing of me strengthened the belief that this project was even worth doing. There aren't enough words to express how much your faith in me mattered.

Erika Chambers, for her unwavering belief that *With Love* matters and needs to be shared with the greater world. Thank you for truly getting me and loving me still.

Julia Blackwell, for literally "fixing my face" in the midst of all the stress of writing this book. Thank you for your long-standing friendship and support to see this project through.

Cindi Barry, for her long-distance love that can be felt across the miles, always. You are the best kind of friend, with support ever present through the decades. Your loyalty is incredibly treasured, and resting in that security is one of the greatest gifts in my life.

Ann Reierson, for being someone with whom my soul can take a deep breath whenever you are present. You are always my example to clients about finding friends who are consistently easy to be around and who help your nervous system to be a lot less nervous.

Suzanne Shellhorn, for being the literal best office neighbor ever and for always being the calm within the storm. Thank you for helping with the front cover project and for being such a steady force in Willow's life and my life.

Acknowledgments

To all my amazing friends, colleagues, and supporters: I am in awe of how many genuinely good people surround me. Thank you for all of your love, encouragement, and support as this project emerged. Your enthusiasm for *With Love* kept me going, each and every day.

My team at Illumify Media for holding my hand in this whole process and for allowing me to write freely and honestly. Michael Klassen, Geoff Stone, and Deb Hall (my *phenomenal* editor)—thank you for your roles in making *With Love* come to life. And to Jen Clark: thank you for being the best sherpa ever and not allowing me to fall down a mountain.

My amazing Title Boxing Club family: because of the environment cultivated at our studio, being able to literally work out the intensity on the bag helped me produce each chapter.

My cherished women's group: you know who you are. It is because of you that I am who I am today, without a shadow of a doubt. Thank you for loving each version of me over the years. It is because of you that I could even write anything in the first place, let alone create a book. Grateful doesn't begin to cut it.

And finally, my beloved Refuge community. Thank you for being the best place to practice vulnerability and authenticity in a real way. If only there were more places like The Refuge, there would be less loneliness, more healing communities, and more brave spaces to speak one's truth. Thank you for being the very first place to practice telling my story out loud.

INTRODUCTION

Mom, I need to tell you something.

I said these words to my mom when I was four. I told her the truth—that my uncle, who was my primary babysitter, was molesting me. Her reaction? That couldn't be true. My response? The beginning of my intentional emotional silence, stubborn determination, and the deep-seated belief that adults were not to be trusted.

Dad, I need to tell you something.

Oh, wait, I don't have a dad to tell anything to. He left when I was three months old, my mother pretending like he didn't exist.

Mom, I need to tell you something.

I want you to know that even after I told you about the horrible things my uncle was doing to me, I am still being abused six years later. It's awful. I'm afraid. I don't feel safe. I'm lonely. I need help. Even if I told another adult, they would go back to my mom, who made me feel much worse and did nothing to protect me anyway.

Stepdad, I need to tell you something.

These words never occurred to me—at ten years old getting a stepdad who was suspicious of this child with no light behind her eyes. He did, however, seek out professional support to discover why this child would hide in her bedroom closet and refused to talk, about really anything. The result of his efforts: my mom placed me in the children's ward of a mental health facility. While I was there, a nurse handed me a form to fill out. Remember, I was only ten years old. I filled out the paperwork myself. One of the questions in the form asked, "Has anyone ever inappropriately touched you? If yes, then who?" Without feeling anything, I answered "Yes." Quite honestly, I didn't think anyone would read it or believe it.

My answer changed the trajectory of my life.

Judge, I need to tell you something.

Being heard for the first time—and subsequently testifying to put my uncle behind bars—helped with the level of injustice, but the solitude of the mental cave I had hunkered down in was far too appealing to vacate it at that point. By then I had created forts with blankets and pillows and soothed myself with the knowledge that no one could disturb me within. Sure, it was terrifying to testify in court, but having mastered the art of dissociation, I wasn't even actually present.

Mom, I need to tell you something.

Your breast cancer is scary. If something happens to you, I'm truly all alone—no brothers, no sisters, no father, no extended family. Alone. After my mom was diagnosed with breast cancer, caring for a deeply depressed tween became overwhelming. So, in her "infinite wisdom," she and my stepdad paid to have me whisked away in the middle of the night and taken to a residential treatment center six hours away in Utah. Please let it be known that the actual "treatment center" was anything but and was a disguised scheme for money laundering and horrific child abuse. While the intention was perhaps genuine, the absolute worst parts of my story occurred during my time there, in ways that are difficult to describe, even now, to my own therapist.

Introduction

Mom, I really need to tell you something.

Even though no words would ever come out describing my year in Utah, even though I still struggle to say them out loud even to my therapist, even though I know they would fall upon deaf ears again, I wish I had had enough safety in the one person who was supposed to keep me safe to tell the truth. Instead, I crawled deeper into my cave, in unbelievable pain but no language to describe it, no grown-ups to protect me. My cave, however, without a shadow of a doubt, saved my sanity, protected me, helped me survive.

I stopped wanting to tell my mom anything.

Returning after a year of torture, malnourishment, and abuse, I created a strategy to keep my access to my cave available but prepare a whole new life, starting from the day I was set free from the Utah prison. I had decided everything would be perfect—my grades, my shiny presentation, my personality. No one can hurt you if there is no reason to be hurt, my young mind thought.

Eventually excelling in academics, speech, and debate in high school, presenting an outgoing and upbeat persona, my adolescence focused entirely on hiding my ever-present internal shame. The fear of being found out constantly lingered, like a dark cloud waiting to burst above me. There was never a safe enough person to spill all the truths that had weighed down my entire childhood. The plan was to go to my grave with what happened, holding tightly to a belief that no one would truly love me if they knew what happened to me. The result: only the walls of the cave held my secrets.

I became a young adult who developed a plethora of both personal and academic achievements as well as a collection of unhealthy coping strategies. My struggles with depression, suicidality, anxiety, disordered eating, addiction, and codependency became avenues that others did not know about. The patterns developed in early childhood perpetuated my tendency to hide, mask, and become secretive in a way that began with hiding myself in the cave.

Had there been a safe therapist who convinced me they could hold my pain—and not also drown—it would have undoubtedly changed the direction of my life. But on the outside, no one knew that was what I needed, and it was also the '90s, so mental health support was not as readily available. Because there was no one guiding me to develop otherwise, my forged pain was deep, complicated, and without insight.

My mom died (ultimately from metastatic breast cancer) when I was in college. Already planning to head to grad school to be a therapist (because let's help other people instead!), the definitive plan was to stay silent about anything in my life pre-high school. It was almost as if the me that lived in the cave never existed and life began at the start of my out-loud success. Never did I reference anything before my freshman year of high school when talking to others, as if I had been dropped off on the planet for grade 9.

Dealing with a gamut of mental health challenges, my intentional strategy was to stuff all the feelings far, far down. In a shocking turn of events, this left me lonely and unable to connect with my friends in meaningful ways.

Friends, I want to tell you something (not really, but I'm going to try).

Over time, it was in my beloved Refuge community that I began to feel safe enough to start revealing myself—my pain, challenges, and needs. Learning through incredible people that the way for real depth, real love, and real connection was actually to be real.

Introduction

Since then, I have been practicing the brutal and intimidating work of unpacking my childhood and adolescence and unlearning all the lessons that outlived their usefulness. My investment in my own therapy pays dividends, as the more integrated a clinician is, the better the support can be subsequently offered to others. One of my deepest desires as a clinician is to help the younger generations suffer far less, live their authentic lives in a way that they do not have to recover from, and find hope and healing that younger me was never given a chance to discover. And she deserved so, so much more than she was given.

Parents, I need to tell you something.

With Love from a Children's Therapist: #lessonsIhavelearnedalongtheway is a true story of emerging from my own broken childhood of utter darkness and sharing the wisdom I've acquired, both as a clinician for two decades as well as a survivor of the unimaginable. This book is evidence of my commitment to the ongoing healing process and my determination to transmute pain into something validating, beneficial, and worthwhile to the greater world.

A wide range of topics can be found within these chapters, and as a therapist for the younger generations, I have selected them as the most valuable. My hope is that the truths found in my story and in my office can help you gather what you need for you and your people, any child you interact with, and for any younger parts of you that may still need to be heard, seen, and deeply understood.

1

#silentnomore

TRAUMA RECOVERY

When we stay silent, they win. I let men silence me. Writing down these stories, I found my voice again.
—June Hart, *The Lost Flowers of Alice Hart*

ONE OF THE MOST IMPACTFUL aspects of recovery has been the ability to talk freely about my story. Shame—an extremely destructive emotion—can control so much of the trajectory of our outlook on ourselves and the world around us. With guilt centering more around what we *do* and shame being a message we believe about who we *are*, my discovery is that the conclusions that we can come to may not always be accurate.

So many kids, teens, and young adults have confided in me over the years about assault, abuse, crime both committed and transgressed upon, regret, beliefs that don't line up with their family values, and numerous other perceived and real infractions. Normalizing the reality of being human—the truth that we are typically never alone in our struggles, with different variables separating us all—is a key healing component.

Ellie, fourteen, came to me via an organization that provides free counseling for suicidal youth. Several months went by before she confided that she was being sexually assaulted by her mom's live-in boyfriend, and it had been going on for years. It was not until she had therapeutic support that she felt safe enough to reveal her reality, and while I am so glad that she did, I hold so much empathy for her about how long she had to endure it alone.

Her mom rallied around her, *until* she expected Ellie to get over it—only two months later. With both words and behavior, her mom's perspective was clear: it was in the past, and why would certain situations be triggering to her? He was out of the home, and she was in weekly counseling.

Sigh.

Unfortunately, this outlook is not unique to Ellie's situation. While we continue to get better at understanding how to be a society with better mental health support, there is not enough education in how to show up for the long story.

Here is what I believe.

People know how to show up for the dramatic rescue.

People know how to show up for the mandated Child Protective Services call.

People know how to show up for the planned intervention.

People know how to show up for the one whole-family session.

But there is a "forever after" when it comes to trauma.

What happens when the girl is an adult and freezes in panic when she is on her back?

What happens when a trigger, unbeknownst to anyone else, gets in the way of typical functioning?

What happens when the child is at their favorite place and sees an abuse scene on replay in their mind?

What happens when a now-adult abuse survivor gets activated by an unrelated event, only to feel small again, like a defenseless child?

What happens if she feels disqualified from having the life she wants because of what she has been through?

What happens when they feel like no one could possibly understand their experience, and they think there is no way out?

Dark stories have the potential to make people feel like impostors in their own lives. There was a time in Utah—when I was assaulted, with neither a chance nor willingness to defend myself—that I didn't want to be a part of my body anymore. The pain was just too much to bear. The shame in thinking I *deserved* that kind of treatment was exponentially more destructive to my sense of self than any of the bruises left behind.

What is wrong with me? I wondered. *Why am I a discarded human, and why am I worth so little that no one is coming to help me?* These thoughts would remain locked up, without being fact-checked by a capable adult.

Three decades later, there is an answer to that plea for help. Someone came, and . . . she was me. I embodied the saying "She needed a hero, so that is what she became." My work with youth is to identify false belief patterns early on that end up perpetuating a negative sense of self. Can you imagine believing so deeply during childhood that you are "enough" that the belief carries you through puberty and adulthood? Me neither, but I just wondered if *you* did.

I know now the way out is through, but believe me, if there was another way, I would have found it. Speaking the truth of what was done to me has proven to be simultaneously brutal as well as astonishingly liberating. The only thing that helps, truly helps, is telling my story in safe spaces—and letting light into the darkness.

Here is what I know, from my own perspective and from listening to twenty years of others' pain: people want to know, "Can you hold it? Will you still love and respect me tomorrow, when I have a vulnerability hangover? Are you able to stay a safe place and allow me room to be human in the process?"

For most of my life, the belief that my story was too intense for others kept me silent. And the truth is, a lot of it just is. My own therapist, Melissa, held space during my moments of panicked hesitation, while I worried that holding the pain would be too much for her. An inner child visualization in our first session hit deep, and as a thoughtful/codependent person, letting her off the hook felt necessary. Naturally, my inclination was to gracefully exit, for I had simply not anticipated the depth of pain left within. However, she voice-messaged me saying, "I am so sorry that anyone ever made you feel like your lived life experiences are too much—or too heavy."

Our work has been crucial in helping me learn to trust that she has not only the safe container available but also the full capacity to hold the hard. Not everyone has earned the rights to our stories, our hearts, our fears, and our pain. Yet the ones we let in are sacred, and we need to be helping our kids not only scan for these people but to *be* these people. Is everyone equipped to hold trauma? Not a chance. Nor is that the expectation or message, but there is a 100 percent guarantee that our friends will go through hard things too—because . . . life. Having kids who don't run away at the first sign of a challenging moment also helps strengthen their own resilience—in an often hostile world.

As clinicians we become equipped people by working through our own pain, with a desire to lead others through—*after* we have trekked through the emotional mud terrain ourselves. Therefore, we need to have an acute awareness of the paths we ourselves have traveled as we receive client populations coming through our doors; we also must recognize when certain situations call for a differently experienced guide. Countertransference is a therapeutic term referring to the internal reaction of a therapist to a client based on their *own* psychological needs. Becoming aware of this possibility needs to be ever present in order to ensure the highest quality of care. Ethically, it is crucial for a clinician to be aware of the boundaries they can emotionally hold space for. No one benefits if a therapist cannot fully hold the tender content vulnerably shared by their brave client. While we cannot predict all of what will show up in the therapeutic space, it is crucial to recognize and honor one's own capacity. In finding support for yourself and/or another, it is my opinion that the best clinicians are actively seeking their own support, supervision, and guidance.

Glennon Doyle states, "Life hurts and it's hard. Not because you're doing it wrong, but because it hurts for everybody. Don't avoid the pain. You need it. It is meant for you."[1]

My amount of challenge has always felt disproportionate to what I imagined others experienced, and it seemed to me like there was some karmic reason why the writer of my story just did not like me. In talking with so many clients over the years, that belief has been reflected back, and so many others feel misunderstood in this life. Younger me felt that if life was some form of cosmic board game, there was either a rule book missing or a level of skill required that I had yet to attain.

But what if the challenges we have been dealt have less to do with who we are and more to do with what we can alchemize them into at the end of the long story? The phrase "This too shall pass" has been both comforting for me and worth mentioning in conversations with people who are suffering. The reality that the intensity of pain subsides and there is an *after* is so helpful in times of acute stress. One of my favorite messages of assurance for kids in counseling is that there's nothing wrong with them and that they have a leg up on mental health because they are talking about the things that everyone else is thinking. Kids share with me they feel different, awkward, alone, confused, pessimistic, and angry.

In asking if they think perhaps anyone else in their school or sports team could also possibly feel those things, soft reassurance begins to soothe where there was once lonely darkness. You mean, it's not just me? Shame dissipates when our shared humanity is normalized. *We are less alone than we think we are.*

Bianca Sparacino, an incredible writer, frames this reality in such a poignant way. "At the end of the day, I want to be proud of the way I turned every loss into a lesson, of the way I believed in light even when I could not see it. At the end of the day, I just want to be proud of the way I connected. I just want to be proud of the person I have become."[2]

It takes incredible bravery to face the memories, chapters, situations, moments that haunt us, no question. Reminding my clients all the time—who are mostly *in* their childhoods—not to spend years burying an issue because it will inevitably return at some point without their permission is so much of our work together. One of my favorite sayings is "If we do not heal what hurt us, we bleed on those who did not cut us." Therefore, it is my highest value to cherish my relationships, support my clients, and continue to do the work, to show up, to heal, and to tell my story.

#silentnomore

2

#olafwithaz

ANXIETY ENTERS THE CHAT

No, you're totally right. That's not going to haunt us for the rest of our lives at all.
—Anxiety, *Inside Out 2*

NINE-YEAR-OLD CAMERON BOUNDED INTO MY playroom, super excited to deliver updated life news that Thursday afternoon. "The doctor put me on new medication for my anxiety problems!" he exclaimed. "Oh, wow. Do you remember what one?" I asked. "YES! It is called, um, Olaf with a *Z*!" #zoloft

Adorable—however, the number of diagnosed children living with anxiety-related disorders has more than skyrocketed in recent years. The COVID-19 pandemic of 2020 also did no favors for kids, especially the ones already struggling with stress-induced challenges. Concerns that never landed on the radar, for adults included, are now woven into the fabric of our thought patterns. Germs alone, from living through the 2020 COVID-19 pandemic, has become the topic of many more conversations than decades prior.

The US Center for Disease Control reported that nearly 15 percent of children ages three to seventeen in America were treated for mental health disorders in 2021, with anxiety being common among school-age children.[3] While many might find these mental health statistics disheartening, it may also be a sign we are paying closer attention to our children. How likely is it that children in previous decades had undiagnosed, overlooked, or masked significant mental health challenges? Incredibly likely.

Parents often ask my opinion of kids and medication, both regarding experiences I've known about as well as the pros and cons of meds. Ethically and legally, as a licensed professional counselor, it is not my lane to advise the use of any medication for depression or anxiety. However, I often strongly encourage people to get their child or teen seen by their primary care doctor or a referred psychiatrist.

And as a mental health professional, my opinions are as varied as my overall client population. Honestly, my daily medication is a gift. In my humble opinion, medication should not necessarily be the very first resort but an option if the current challenges are far surpassing one's literal ability to think clearly. While there is a concern for the developing brain of a child, I would also chime in that a level of persistent and pervasive anxiety is negatively impacting healthy development if left unchecked for a long duration. Watching a child who is so sad they cannot get out of bed, or a teenager too anxious to make friends, begin to live life again with even a small dosage of extra medical help is incredible to witness.

When one's struggle far surpasses their capacity to cope, my inclination is to use every resource possible for survival. As someone who has battled major depressive disorder, I know that medication, combined with a healing community and therapeutic support, saved my life. However, the chemical cocktail of antidepressants and sleep medication is not enough to fight through the memories terrorizing many who live with trauma. When the memories crash over me like a tidal wave, the idea of making it all stop is incredibly alluring. It makes sense to me when teens tell me they just want to turn their brain completely off forever. In those moments, it is evident that medication is not fully sufficient, as sadness does not completely vanish with the pills. However, medications increase the production of brain chemicals that have been depleted due to coping with heavy circumstances. The intensity would be too much to bear for so many without the medicine dulling some of the edges of the trauma.

Passive suicidal ideation involves feelings and thoughts about wanting to die, without the actual planning to follow through with a suicide attempt. More than any other factor, chronic anxiety is associated with heightened suicidal thoughts. Left unchecked, it may transform into even more active suicidal ideation. People who deal with panic attacks regularly often feel hopeless and exhausted—and, ironically, panicked that a panic attack can arrive with little notice.

Here's the biology of a panic attack, in hopefully the most succinct lesson ever: Your hypothalamus, which manages your body temperature, sends messages through the carrier of your autonomic nervous system to the adrenal glands, which regulate your response to stress. That memo prompts them to spam the bloodstream with hormones such as adrenaline and cortisol, the stress hormone. The chemical messengers engage the system's survival reflexes and set the body on the defense. Your body becomes fully prepared to save your life at all costs.

Often, my anxiety description to kids is this: There is a little person in your brain, and their job is to help warn you if a tiger is coming to attack. The problem, though, is there is rarely ever an actual tiger. So the little guy in the brain needs to be thanked for his service but gently go away for some vacation time. He can be on call if needed, but it is likely he can truly take an extended leave of absence. Olive, ten, was dealing with racing, anxious thoughts impacting her ability to enjoy time with her friends. She kept feeling the panicked need to run away, so time spent with them was rapidly decreasing. We called the overly enthusiastic employee in her head Reggie so she could easily call him by name. "Reggie! You are okay! We are having fun and we are safe. Take a break already!" When some of this inner work happens in times without extreme stress, it becomes less difficult to prepare oneself for panicked moments.

For those perhaps not familiar with the Pixar *Inside Out* series, let me introduce you to kid therapist movie gold. (Moderately obsessed? Perhaps.) *Inside Out* is an animated film featuring a young girl named Riley; the movie shows her emotions playing characters operating her brain's control panel. When *Inside Out 2* came out this year, Riley, now thirteen, is dealing with more complicated emotions than the original Joy, Sadness, Anger, Disgust, and Fear. The character Anxiety stars as a main role in the sequel, orchestrating thoughts in Riley's mind to eliminate suffering—by always being several steps ahead. The irony of the plot includes Anxiety spinning out of control in her frantic attempt to make things run efficiently. Riley has a full-blown panic attack, her thoughts consuming her mind. Anxiety ends up saying sadly in defeat, "I'm sorry. I was just trying to protect her."[4]

This protective response is the true essence of understanding anxiety. Conversations happened in my office for months after the movie came out about this pivotal scene, focusing on how Anxiety is *not* the villain. Many clients come to me frustrated and ashamed, believing anxiety is ruining their lives. When anxiety is consuming so much of their mental energy, it makes sense why they feel so exasperated. Kids will often manifest psychosomatic reactions (headaches, tummy troubles) connected to emotional pain. As C. S. Lewis stated, "It is easier to say, 'My tooth is aching,' than it is to say, 'My heart is broken.'"[5]

Anxiety Enters the Chat

So many young people have come to me believing something is deeply wrong with them due to the way their brain works. Clients enter my office with all types of challenges, including weather anxiety (common in the Rocky Mountain region here I live), social anxiety, selective mutism, fear of large crowds, driving, medical procedures, and the list goes on.

An important designation: diagnosed anxiety differs from our everyday challenges and worries. Invalidation can result when a person dealing with debilitating anxiety is reminded that "everyone worries sometimes." Yes, this is true. Worry is often a motivator in our capitalistic society to make sure that everyone is doing what they need in order to keep things moving along. (*The Busy World of Richard Scarry* TV series taught us this early on. What a world.)

Standard worry significantly differs, however, from someone being paralyzed with fear after being put in a similar situation as their trauma. Often, I say, "Help me understand more of what it is like to be you." Just because someone else also doesn't like closed spaces does not necessarily mean that I know how that fear lands in *their* mind and body. Synergetic Play Therapy, or SPT, the model embodied in my practice, primarily uses attunement to key into how the child *right in front of me* may feel. Panic attacks related to trauma are normal responses to abnormal scenarios. The nervous system is doing its original job—helping to keep a person safe. Helpful options for my clients have been to adopt mantras as gentle, repeated reminders that soon become automatic. *I am safe in my body. I am protected. I am loved.*

My anxiety is trying to help me.

In addition to all the other things kids and teenagers worry about, including checking the ratio of online time a crush had before responding to a message, they also have extreme challenges that youth of two decades ago did not. The prevalence of school shootings is more than beyond alarming, and without getting too political, my heart breaks every time an act of preventable violence takes place.

Talking to kids all week long about their "bad shooter" drills and strategies that schools have in place to keep students safe while attending fourth grade is beyond how I experienced elementary school. We are living in a different time, where kids tell me they plan their wardrobe not to be too brightly colored and therefore easily spotted, or where teens pick electives that won't be close to the main entrance of their school to help reduce their risk of dying in the event of a school shooting.

"Not super sure why I feel afraid all the time. I'm worried that my anxiety has come back," said one of my teenage clients on a random Thursday. "It's possible," I said. "Or also true—that you go to school in America?"

Lisa Dion, founder of Synergetic Play Therapy, in her podcast *Lessons from the Playroom*, spoke about the reality of preparing kids for this modern world in which we live. In episode 29 from May 2018, "Helping Children and Parents When Tragedy Strikes," Lisa says, "We can't promise to keep kids safe from tragedy, but we can promise to have a plan."

A safety plan, the most controllable of all options, can be a great resource when the world, or a child's world, feels out of control. Even smaller changes can make a big difference to a person dealing with an overwhelming sense of anxiety. This weekend, for instance, I am joining a group of my friends for dinner and a comedy show. My felt sense of safety increases when my seat is close to the end of the aisle. To some, this may not seem like a meaningful choice, but to me, one who has experienced being trapped over and over, having agency over being able to leave suddenly if needed feels like freedom.

My anxiety is trying to help me.

Often witnessed in my office is the marriage of the aftermath of an anxiety attack and shame. So much of my work is normalizing realities and helping kids see they are not the first person to have ever experienced some of what they are moving through. As Brené Brown wisely explained, "Shame corrodes the very part of us that believes we are capable of change. What we don't need in the midst of struggle is shame for being human. Empathy is a connection; it is a ladder out of the shame hole."[6] My consistent observation, in the two decades of being a clinician, and years prior working with youth in non-profit organizations, is that across the board of personality types, kids want to know: Do you understand me? Hearing "You make sense" can resonate as so comforting, as it makes the desire to be seen relatable.

My anxiety is trying to help me.

While there are therapeutic interventions to manage anxiety, additional comfort can be found in creating strategies that buffer a sense of control. For me, there are multiple things that I choose not to engage in. What would be helpful to remind ourselves and our friends or kids who struggle is that there is no way to avoid life altogether without missing the good stuff. A teenager shared that she was afraid of a boy's rejection, and we talked about how part of the journey is finding someone to share a meaningful connection with. Also, we discussed how the made-up plotlines in movies are likely all inaccurate, causing unnecessary suffering.

In a similar vein, traumatized kids need to be reminded that having a panic attack after trauma doesn't make them defective, unlovable, or unworthy—it makes them human.

Restoring our sense of safety is step one, and making sure that we have places and people who are truly safe is crucial in the development of new neural pathways. Those with complex trauma have had their internal sense of safety destroyed, and new habits need to be formed to resurrect a sense of self that is conducive to a regulated nervous system. Helping our kids look for signs of safety in times when they are not in danger can help their neural pathways begin to develop the ability to do so easily. "How do you know you are safe?" is an excellent question to help a sense of awareness and connectedness to this time and place. When we are in an anxious head space, our mind is either in the past or the future—neither of which is as beneficial as being in the here and now.

One of my favorite interventions is the creation of a sensory grounding kit. We brainstorm ideas for all five of their senses and try to pick things that will give them an instant sense of comfort and relief. Olfaction, our sense of smell, is the fastest sense to reach the brain, because smell signals go directly to the olfactory bulb. NYU School of Medicine published a study that showed it takes less than one-tenth of a second for the sense of smell to distinguish between odors.[7] For this reason, when we make kits in my office, I encourage my clients to find a scent they find soothing.

The smell of sandalwood is an incredibly comforting scent for me and helps orient me to the present day. So, in an intentional practice to regulate my own nervous system, I often light a sandalwood-scented candle each night before bed. Clients and I brainstorm *their* soothing options, and together we form a kit and a plan for times of angst, utilizing their five senses. While a comfort kit is not a magic cure, the hope is that it helps return a person back to their body, so that logic has a chance to catch up. This weekend, I am making sensory comfort kits with The Refuge tweens and teens as part of my empowerment series of coffee shop hangouts. We will be talking about what it means to be on solid ground, and someone will inevitably make a joke about being grounded (already laughing, kids, ha-ha.) Various forms of fidget toys, soft fabrics, and scented items will be available to help them redirect when stress inevitably shows up, you know, like every day? Also, it is never a bad idea to include a note reminding your person that you are there for them, that you're not going anywhere. Words of affirmation are also an immediate balm to anxious hearts.

We need patience, grace, anxiety education, coping skills, and the willingness to see our people to the other side of fear, as their freedom awaits. Anxiety is not the enemy; rather, it can be repurposed as a superpower to help.

And as a final reminder: your anxiety is trying to help you.

#olafwithaz

3

#denyingthedragon
THE REALITY OF SUICIDALITY

You are not the darkness you endured.
You are the light that refused to surrender.
—John Mark Green

AT FACE VALUE, WE MAKE a lot of both accurate as well as incorrect assumptions about people, instantly and on a consistent basis. Elementary education guides us in this type of critical thinking, in fact—with pictures that ask us to explain what Bob or Jane is feeling or what is happening in the context of the presented story. I remember indignantly thinking as a child, *Uh, I am not those people? How could I possibly hear inside their brains?* Evolutionary psychology tells us, however, that this behavioral analysis makes sense, as our very ancestors based their survival on observations, you know, to avoid being eaten by bears or wolves. Thanks to them for learning that for us, though, truly.

However, we often have opportunities when we find out we are wrong, and this is the case for so many clients, friends, and people that I speak with, including myself. Today, in fact, a fourteen-year-old client said to me, in reference to my relating to her own deep depression, "*You* get really sad sometimes too?" Um, yes. One of my primary motivations for creating this book is to integrate my life stories and bridge the gap between my challenges and the professional face I present to the world. While everything experienced isn't up for grabs, there is plenty of processed content ready to be repackaged for my clients and my readers.

The hope of helping others feel less alone, teens more actually understood, and grown-ups of kids potentially gaining more insight now outweighs the desire to stay quiet in my deep inner world. The cost of remaining silent is simply too high.

Authenticity, as mentioned, is one of my highest values, and yet we cannot share what hurts so deeply—at least in a way that is truly helpful—without having done the hard work first. Nadia Bolz-Weber once stated profoundly, "If you're going to share widely, make sure that you're sharing from your scars and not your open wounds."

In my eighteen years of private practice in Colorado as well as a year and a half working in community mental health, my estimate is that several hundred depressed and suicidal youth in the Colorado area have entered my office doors. When I worked at Community Reach Center, I was hired for the Adolescent Intensive Outpatient team, where 100 percent of the admitted kids were actively suicidal and often in extremely challenging life situations.

As a current provider for Second Wind Fund, providing free counseling to uninsured or underinsured kids and teens at risk of suicide, I have heard story after story of darkness, wanting to leave the world and finding existence pointless. While my heart aches for each of them and the intensity in which depression smothers a life, the benefit of naming the invisible dragon out loud remains the boldest voice in the room.

My own interpretation of the metaphorical monster of suicidality is equivalent to the scaly and gigantic body of a dragon. While there are numerous envisioned versions, the symbol rings true to me after years and years of hearing about depressive symptoms. I talk to kids every week who are haunted by something huge they cannot see, find difficult to describe, and don't feel like they can share with many outside a therapy office. Because who would honestly believe a mythological creature is tormenting them and keeping them trapped within a castle of their own creation? But what if we were able to externalize the depression in a way that made it easier to battle? What if we saw our kids needing both internal resolve as well as support from external soldiers to help defeat the dragon attacking their castle? What if we remembered to include in the narrative that we are a person *experiencing* depression, as opposed to depression making up our identity? Would there be less shame and stigma in admitting we need help if our perspective shifted focus to a dilemma rather than a defect? Perhaps.

Years ago, I confided over lunch to my dear friend Carolyn, a brilliant social worker, about sometimes having really dark, depressive thoughts. She looked at me over her salad and said, "I wish there was a way we could all just be more honest about it. In the counseling world, so many suffer alone because they are too ashamed of the stigma to talk about it." We all need a Carolyn. Systemically, there is a lot of shame in the mental health field among clinicians who have struggles, although therapists are technically not exempt from being human. Technically.

When truth be told, the more our wounds are acknowledged and dealt with, the more we can empathize and support others. As a licensed mental health professional, it's hard for me to share when things feel bleak, so empathizing with a tween who feels so sad, but who doesn't have the ability to articulate exactly how, comes naturally. We want to deny the sadness, so kids are told to get fresh air, exercise, find a hobby, make better friends, break up with certain friends, stop playing video games, put down the phone, start a different fixation, read a book, count your blessings, and it will all be fine. While those suggestions do hold value, each to varying degrees, behind all of this I would add a dark reminder: suicidality knows no limits in terms of whom depression can impact. Someone can be desperately trying to do all the "right things" and still deeply struggle with depression. Again, depression is an absolute beast. Forgetting that no population is immune renders all the other ideas fairly meaningless, especially if we only offer platitudes and clichés when perhaps more is needed.

The line—which all my clients know—whether one is forced to put a suicidal person in the hospital is the intent of a plan. This mandate remains in effect to keep people alive and has assuredly saved so many lives. Suicidal ideation is a range of wishes, thoughts, and preoccupations with death and suicide: a huge portion of the standard things I listen to in my office.

I welcome it.

Here's a debunked myth: if kids talk about suicide, ideas will form in their heads, and they are more likely to act upon it. False. The ideas are already there, so naming the messages that come from the dragon—*You will never amount to anything. The world would be better off without you. You are a waste of space*—gives an opportunity that was not there before for another person to speak truth to the lies that the dragon spews.

If we don't know about the verbal violence that is taking place in a teenager's head, how in the world are we to dialogue in a way that proves redemptive? If kids don't feel like there is safe space to be able to verbalize those thoughts, the feelings will not simply dissipate into the night. They won't.

When I was fourteen years old, I intentionally attempted to end my life with an entire bottle of my mom's cancer pills (she had a pharmacy's worth) in my room, after a speech and debate tournament. One would think, perhaps, that I hadn't performed as well as I wanted to, and my actions were in response to the outcome. Well, in a way, yes—except that it was my very first tournament as a new team member, and I had won the entire competition's all-around title.

Plagued with shameful memories, actively shoving them down so deep without air at the surface, the pain remained, and the dichotomy inside was simply too much to bear. Emotional language was lacking, so I did not have the ability or support to communicate the inner turmoil. While everyone was giving me a standing ovation in a packed auditorium, the very soul of me was still cowering, still feeling violated and repulsive, wishing the earth would swallow me whole. Sure, I clean up well, but the internal damage ran so deep that no accolades or medals or admiration could comfort the wounded child that deserved to be held and rocked.

Denying the darkness altogether meant accepting the praise of my delighted team, leaving with two armfuls of trophies, and going home with the intent to make the fire inside extinguish for good. My parents were at the hospital at the time, so my plan was to exit and never look back. They came home early, though, and my mom walked into my room already talking about a bathroom chore and saw me crumpled in a heap on my bed with the empty pill bottle. She began screeching about how she was the one in pain with a diagnosis, slapped my face over and over, had my stepdad call 911, and yelled about how *cancer* was something to die about. To be fair, that had to be an alarming sight to see your only child desperately trying to leave this life. And let me tell you, I wanted the pain to be over more than I could articulate. There

The Reality of Suicidality

didn't seem to be another way to move forward, because at fourteen, in agony without a trusted adult, one comes to their own conclusions, as twisted as they may be. Those were the days of getting your stomach pumped with charcoal (horrendous, let me tell you), being put on a mandated hold, and getting legally whisked to the hospital via ambulance.

As soon as I realized my attempt was unsuccessful, my immediate default was to drastically course correct, and I began flipping into a shiny, happy, "just kidding, I'm fine" version of myself. She was much more armored and together, much less of anything dark or sad. She'd found the error of her ways, and of course everyone gets sad sometimes. Yes, maybe I will take a week break from the competition team. I will take deep breaths and go on walks and be okay enough for everyone around me to go back to their business—later earning state and national titles, team MVP and Most Reliable awards, all while pushing down the pain as far as possible. Nope, no time for that.

Spoiler alert: I was *absolutely* not okay. And true to my family of origin's nature, it was never ever talked about again. Not once. We were all relieved to not have to go there—the problem was, the pain didn't vanish. Instead, it was just shoved further down, so that excavation when enough emotional safety was in place became more brutal, buried under years of masking and unhealthy ways to cope.

My firm belief is that so many die by suicide because they are not sure how to ask for help, how not to freak their people out, how not to make things weird moving forward. Had there been someone safe to talk to, my internal battle would not have felt like a solo mission. It made more sense to me just to leave than to try to figure out how to start asking for help. In fact, the devasting irony is that everything is sad and weird and horrible when someone you love dies by suicide.

Let me be very clear: suicide is an incredibly complex issue, and there is no one blanket-statement analysis that fully covers each precious life. However, in my experience, there are elements of truth that may resonate, and the desire is to help connect the dots in as many ways as possible, for as many people as possible. My family of origin was ill-equipped (obviously) to support me, and therefore, my respect runs deep for any parent or adult who wants to know a better way to help a child heal. Even choosing this book out of potential curiosity gives me hope that there are adults who consider the mental health of a child to be a worthwhile priority.

What if we created a world in which the conversation around depression and suicidality was more normalized and we had more support around creating better containment for our kids? Robbie's Hope is a grassroots nonprofit organization that started in Jefferson County, Colorado, where my office resides. Their mission is to create an uprising of teens talking to other teens, to stop the suicide epidemic. They do so much in our community, fighting hard to communicate that "It is okay to not be okay" and making sure peer support is available. Suicide remains the number one cause of death in teenagers in Colorado.

Saying "You have dark thoughts *too*? I thought I was the only one" is a beautiful beginning to shedding light into an area that was too full of stigma to explore alone. In addition, another way we can shift things is to eliminate the use of comparative suffering. Often people say, "But you have everything?" or "You have it better than X." This only serves to shame and force a greater sense of reluctance in already hurting people to ask for support. There is always room to help shine light in the darkness, but in my experience, the approach of "What? You seem to be doing just fine; look on the bright side" never seems to be effective.

The Reality of Suicidality

One of my Spotify playlists is titled #whendarknessshowsup, which contains songs that remind me to hold on, move forward, and know that pain eventually ends. I often challenge my clients to make a playlist of instant mood boosters with songs that have no negative associations for them. For me, when things feel heavy, reminders are needed that everything isn't terrible in the world and music remains a constant. This appears to be the case for so many, as music offers us language when our own emotions drown out the beauty of the sun. When my abuse happened in Utah, I repeated Pearl Jam's "Black" song lyrics to myself about one day having a beautiful life (entirely out of context, I realize, but powerful nonetheless), one day being a star in another sky. And let me tell you: I held on to that verse like a lifeline, repeating it over and over while the abuse was happening. It gave me a focus, reminding me that this agony could not and would not last forever.

The belief that there was an after, a beyond the pain, a tomorrow that held the hope of something different than the hell I was experiencing as a child carried me into having the next moments. That song still offers me support by speaking to a deep part of me that has always needed to be understood.

Without being too graphic, it is important to note there were numerous instances where my life was threatened in Utah. As it happened on multiple occasions, I began, somehow, to manufacture a different relationship with death. Pretending I was already somewhere safe became second nature. Hearing Lin Manuel Miranda's line in *Hamilton* about imagining death so much it felt like a factual memory made me tremble with familiarity as an adult. My entire being resonated with the truth of those lyrics, an example of how unprocessed memory can haunt the present.

Many of our youth are experiencing false interpretations of what beyond this life can mean. They express to me a paradise awaits, with no more pain ever. Sure, *of course* it sounds appealing. But as I said to a teenager this week, "What if you are wrong? What if there is a beyond this pain in *this* life and you are denying yourself the opportunity to ever find out? What if you are missing out on people you will love, concerts you would have experienced, places you have never been, moments of joy you never thought possible? That would suck, yeah?"

One of my first community mental health intakes: a teenager who tried to die by drinking a bottle of bleach. It is as awful as it sounds and, for the record, incredibly ineffective. In talking with her, she indicated no one would care if she even lived. Now, while there were some alarming challenges in her family of origin, we talked about other ways of finding support and connection to defeat that destructive thought pattern. The poisonous message had existed in her head long before she acted out her plan, because no one knew. And if no one has a clue, there is also zero chance for anyone to help.

The people in our lives need to know we are glad they exist, that the world would not be better off without them, that they matter as unique individuals in this world, and how our lives are fuller because of their existence. We assume our people know these things, and yet when it comes down to it, there is no downside to making sure they are verbally told on more than one occasion. In my experience, the opposite, damaging core messages are the lies that reign in the inner caves of minds and cannot survive exposure.

As one who has battled major depressive disorder, I know firsthand that brains can go offline, and when they do, nothing makes sense. This is where we need our people—to help us see the world clearly again. As I was explaining to a teen regarding her depressive episodes, it is as if our brain's Wi-Fi gets disconnected or the password has suddenly been changed. We do not have access in the same way to our wisdom, so instead of begrudging the lack of service, it is time to be creative to get our needs met, including borrowing connection from a friend's network. Using the language of the people, really.

One of my most favorite social media influencers, Elyse Myers, speaks so beautifully about her journey with recovery and mental health. Her words continue to hold free real estate in my brain: "Every day I wake up is another day I never planned on having and sometimes have to convince myself to keep having. Every single day I chose to stay I have been given the opportunity to age. Every good thing I experience is so bittersweet because I am reminded that I almost didn't experience it. And it is so f*&^% good, that I am so glad I stuck around for it. It's worth sticking around for, I promise."[8]

Defeating the metaphorical dragon isn't about denying his existence. For as much as we would like him not to show up, pretending not to see him is not the path to conquering the irritating monster. Triumph over depression means looking the beast straight into his menacing eyes and saying, "I'm going to talk about you. I'm going to be honest about what I see when I feel you trying to call me into the fire, and I'm going to let my people help extinguish the intensity of the flames, and that . . . *that* is how you will lose your power."

#denyingthedragon

4

#needymcneedersonpants
NEEDS WELCOMED HERE

People who need people are the luckiest people in the world.
—*Funny Girl*

EVERY JANUARY, MANY OF MY friends participate in the "Word of the Year" activity. The idea is to focus on a word that helps center and remind you of your goals for the year. My 2024 word was *integrate*, and the heart of the choice was this project. I wanted to integrate the reality of my story with the wisdom from behind the scenes, creating a book of value for others.

Integration is literally defined in the Cambridge Dictionary as "combining two or more things to become more effective." Cultivating an entire life focused on service and being useful to others has also included at times denying the parts of me that I deemed too dark, too ugly, and too unacceptable to be part of the reality I present to the world. But becoming more whole means embracing the entire story and allowing duality to coexist.

It became time in 2011 to start integrating both, and I finally began the process of opening up about the tragic "missing" year of my life, and I soon began to feel freer. In 2016, I participated in the Denver tour of This Is My Brave, which is a nonprofit to empower individuals to put names to true stories of recovery from mental illness. It was the first time I spoke publicly about my journey with major depressive disorder and post-traumatic stress syndrome. Healing in more ways than one, my video has been a catalyst for me to become more known in my relationships, often paving the way to deeper conversations.

In the process of writing this book, it has become absolutely and completely necessary to acknowledge the truth that the things that were done to me need to be spoken about, finally.

Resistance, with whom I previously shared a metallic best friend's locket, had become a force holding me back from feeling the freedom that awaited on the other side of honesty. My dear friend Nikki is a trauma therapist, incredible human, and someone you want on your team. Nikki has trauma around lightning, as she was literally struck by it one awful day years ago. In talking with her, though, Nikki is very clear about what she needs. When our friends with a boat want to go out on the water on a day that is potentially stormy, Nikki declines. Nikki doesn't think twice about saying what she needs or feels, and I deeply admire my assertive friend, who tells it like it is. Nikki, in fact, would be encouraging me to speak the truth, regardless of what anyone else will do or say, clients and client parents included.

For me, as a consummate Enneagram 2, my core motivation is to be loved and also, in an unhealthy sense, to avoid acknowledging my own needs. As a young child, I was being sexually abused by my uncle, who was my primary babysitter for my single mom. When I needed her the most, when I told her at age three that I had been touched, she had an explosive, negative, shaming reaction. She denied that could be a thing and raged the rest of that Sunday as she angrily clipped coupons from the paper. (Fine. But at age six, I flushed my aunt's wedding ring down the toilet, to make divorce happen. Apparently, it does not work that way?)

The abuse continued for seven.more.years.

That is the last time I distinctly recall as a child asking for *anything* I needed.

My first-grade teacher, Mrs. Somersall, noticed I was not reacting to the words on the chalkboard in class. As an extremely compliant child, this was an obvious flag for my teacher, who told my mom that she suspected something was wrong with my eyesight.

Taken to the eye doctor, I proudly received my very first pair of blue Smurfette-themed glasses. To this day, I wear an extreme, near-blind prescription of contacts, without which the world looks too blurry for me to function. Six-year-old me had also known something was wrong, but I was *already* far too afraid to ask for anything. There was also never a sick day for me, in my elementary school years. (Perfect attendance awards every year, baby!)

A former therapist tilted her head when I mentioned never being sick as a child, and she responded, "From what you know of kids, does that sound normal to you?" In my mom's defense, she was a single parent, and our social system is not set up to accommodate solo working parents. Knowing it was never an option to miss school, I just didn't voice any reason to. However, I believed until only recently that I was just immune from getting sick. (Pun absolutely intended.)

Granted, I recognized my mom's parenting left much to be desired and hoped her reaction was far less common than the necessary support, nurturing, and safety children deserved. In fact, a part of me heals every time a parent tells me they wish their kid would just verbalize what they need, or I hear my parent friends talk about how hard it is to watch their teen grow up and, while natural, to have their kids need

Needs Welcomed Here

them less. While I recognize, after seeing so many families over the years, that my experience was not the norm, it creates an opportunity to speak to the gap between what was and what could be. The icebreaker question "Would you rather be wanted or needed?" always used to be met with, "Obvi—needed." Now, as an adult continuing to grow and heal, the beauty is clearly apparent being wanted too.

Considering one of the most significant core memories of my childhood, I beg of you—please don't cultivate an environment in which your child is too ashamed or too afraid of rejection or too proud to say, "Please help me." On numerous occasions, I invite a parent into the session when there is something they should know, and we need their assistance to make it happen. Addison, nine, was being verbally and emotionally bullied and manipulated in secret—by the tween of family friends. She did not want to speak up and risk her parents' friendship being strained. It was important for her to understand that our basic needs for safety and respect are nonnegotiable and that being treated the way she had been was unacceptable.

We talked about her parents' relationship with the bully's parents not being her responsibility, and if things continued to escalate, it would simply make things even more complicated. Codependent behaviors include prioritizing others' needs before your own, and breaking that pattern before it becomes a habit is an honor to witness in young kids. How much energy would that have saved for me to absorb that lesson as a preteen? You too?

Please do not intentionally (no one gets it right all the time) shame your child for wanting/asking/needing something. Conversation is one thing; using blaming language will always put a person on the defense and create the necessity to hide. "You always need to be alone after school and don't want to talk to me!" is a common complaint that kids tell me is thrown to them from adults. Time and time again, kids explain that school is so draining (so many people), and they would prefer to recharge (alone) rather than be irritable—and then get in trouble for being irritable.

Sure, there is something to be said about entitlement and requests that surpass basic limitations of what one can provide, but my hope is that we can continue to grow into people who have fewer emotional land mines attached to our conversations. Often, behaviors we take for granted as adults can be seen as simply unacceptable in kids. Who doesn't have a grumpy attitude sometimes? I mean, other than me?

We all need to be seen, heard, and validated for who we really are, with no loopholes. If we wish to narrow down the needs of kids, in my opinion, they would be funneled into these three umbrellas of support:

Seeing them for who they are, not who we think they should be.

Hearing their views and perspectives on life and their current sense of reality.

Validating their emotions, regardless of what *we* think they should be feeling.

Who wants to be told how to feel anyway? And furthermore, who actually experiences the emotion we are told to have?

One of my thirteen-year-old clients, Abbie, shared that her mom, trying to connect, had giggled asking her if she had any crushes. Abbie, way more into her sport, school, and fantasy fiction to have room for boys, tried to tell her about a book character she found interesting. Abbie's mom rolled her eyes and walked away in a huff; the message that my client hadn't responded *correctly* was heard loud and clear. Abbie cried to me in session, "See? I can't say anything right, and she wonders why I don't ever want to talk to her. That's why."

We *all* want to be truly known and deserve people and places that facilitate that sense of knowing.

The problem that I see, day in and day out, is that kids/teens/young adults/humans report no one wanting to hear their stories. All day long: conversations filled with deep shame, guilt, distorted thinking, confusion, eating disorders, abuse, harmful decisions, self-harm, broken relationships, and people simply feeling all alone in their struggles.

I will often ask, "Who else knows about this? Who in your world can support you in this journey?" And time and time again, the answer is, "Just you."

Let me be very clear: having a good therapist is just not enough.

Yes, my role as a clinician is cherished. Therefore, I continue to work incredibly hard to become a better version of myself and heal so that I can also help my clients better. The line "You can't take people further than you have been willing to go yourself" is a badge of honor—and why I invest in my healing work to help as many people as possible.

However.

At best, my clients see me once a week, and some, every other week. Even for clients in crisis, who have on occasion been seen for two sessions per week, a fifty-minute session to vent out an entire week's worth of challenges, while leaving room for feedback is not enough time.

Life happens rapidly, and having safe places to land throughout the week for my clients is incredibly comforting. If a client must wait until the next Tuesday to talk to me, I am incredibly happy to hear that Tony the youth pastor was able to support the teenager in a hard moment. Or that the safe aunt came over and got to have a meaningful conversation. We need safe friends, coaches, teachers, mentors who can stand in the gap and do life with us and love us through our story.

For the past seventeen years, I have been part of a private women's group that has been nothing short of transformative in my adult life. In the beginning, my personal sharing was fairly guarded, at best, but over time it has become a place each month to talk about what is really going on and gather strength for the weeks ahead. And this group is as real as it gets, and I feel grateful to have a safe space to cry, question, laugh, celebrate, mourn, love and be loved. It is a million times easier to listen than to talk, and yet . . . *Practice what you preach, Stacy.*

These women have modeled authentic storytelling in a genuine circle of trust and shown me what it means to truly witness and love the different versions of ourselves as we become them.

I have felt like I have served a literal lifetime in protection services against My Past to save my friends from feeling any of the pain I have endured. Our kids need to share these stories in real time so as not to collect interest from years of buried words. We all have needs, yet when they are *not acknowledged*, they become problematic and then burdensome.

What I have learned, albeit slowly, is that the intensity of what we endure does not gush out from us with the same force in which the stories were lived. Rather, the burden of holding the toxins within my body dissipates when someone else holds space for the pain to come out. There are so many reasons why this formula is effective, and as one who was never good at math can attest to, I am incredibly grateful.

#needymcneedersonpants

5

#truthbombs
BITE-SIZED SNIPPETS

Whatever truth we feel compelled to withhold, no matter how unthinkable it is to imagine ourselves telling it, not to is a way of spiritually holding our breath. You can only do it for so long.
—Mark Nepo

ONE OF MY MOST FAVORITE things is to attend Broadway musicals at our local performing arts theater. Kathy, my honorary mom, has made it a tradition of taking me to a performance for my birthday, and it is seriously the best quality time gift ever. Now, I will take any chance to have the privilege of attending a show, sometimes even twice if it is fantastic.

Jagged Little Pill, the musical based solely on Alanis Morissette's lyrics, was one of the most powerful shows I have ever seen. The entire premise is based on an intense fictional (but based on reality) story, fitting perfectly with her most popular songs. Not shying away from so many controversial topics, the main themes are drug abuse and sexual assault, with additional coverage all over the map including plenty of other options for heavy discussion.

For me, the significance of a repressed sexual assault resurfacing decades later after someone else's current date rape was not lost on me. Trying not to sob loudly outright, I felt my whole body get the chills as the actress playing high schooler Bella, the one who had been assaulted, sang "No."

She sang about sitting with secrets that she was no longer willing to hold. Louder, she inquired, wondering how the word *no* was not understood?

I was flooded and overwhelmed with so many internal reactions, wanting to be alone, but settled for the restroom directly after the show. However, a poignant moment happened in the women's bathroom that will stick with me forever. While I was in a stall, a girl said out loud to anyone who was listening, "Does *anyone else* think that it is so messed up that *so many* of us related to that for the *wrong* reasons?"

Instantly, I piped up, "Yep!" from behind my door, and a chorus of various voices of agreement pinged from the bathroom tiles, in an incredible number of responses. "Yes" and "Me too" and "Yeah" rang devastatingly clear.

Truth: the anonymity of the public bathroom, where there will never be follow-up to responses shared behind stall walls, may be the closest some ever get to sharing their stories.

This is a deep societal tragedy.

While there could have been attendance at an after-show pop-up group therapy event, the intensity in that bathroom was completely palpable. We need more opportunities to be raw, real, and seen. The crisis centers are always flooded with group requests, and you can't just order online a safe circle of friends with express shipping. (That would be *super* convenient, though.) One of the hopes of this book is to create conversations about how we can show up in relationships that we are in. How we can be more open about the realities of living in a world with so much violence and share our real stories with one another. In all honesty, some of my friends reading first drafts of this book didn't yet know some of my dark stories. Our connections have been forged deeper because of conversations surrounding these experiences.

If You Really Knew Me was a 2010 MTV reality show I loved that didn't make me cringe or feel uncomfortable watching someone's relationship fall apart. The premise was focused on youth subculture and cliques in different high schools, and they chose applicant schools with high rates of issues like cyberbullying or division in the student population. Challenge Day, after lots of intentional icebreakers and laughs, was when they separated the teens into strategic groups with an adult leader. Finishing the sentence "If you really knew me" included incredibly powerful disclosures, where students quickly learned how much they had in common. The purpose was to change the way the students saw themselves, their school, and each other. It was incredibly effective.

I often wonder, if I'd had a quality therapist at age sixteen, someone who could've truly held my pain, how would that have shifted the very trajectory of my life? Would I have been able to tell her that, like Bella in *Jagged Little Pill*, I felt so much deep shame at being the center of abuse, night after night? Would I have been able to ask for support even about how to consider one day having a romantic relationship after enduring such humiliation? Would I have so many fewer challenges, since my developmental process was built on a premise of solidly covering the original foundation?

Would I have had so much less struggle working to integrate the pieces of my story into my adult life, perhaps able to make a mosaic of meaning sooner rather than later?

The truth here is that so many things are only first spoken behind therapy office doors. My friends who are therapists for adults can attest to people coming in their doors for a first-time reveal of something significant . . . from childhood.

My often-repeated line is, "My job is to prevent less disturbed adults."

Parents often call me for an initial appointment and immediately exclaim, "I think I screwed up my kid!" My response is always the same: "Well, they are being raised by humans, so . . ." It takes an incredible amount of humility to bring your child/teen to a therapist and say, "Please help. I don't know what to do."

As my mentor, the brilliant Lisa Dion, founder of the Synergetic Play Therapy Institute, once stated in a conference workshop, "No one looks at their newborn when they are placed into their arms at the hospital and says, 'I can't *wait* to take you to therapy.' Be gentle with parents."[9] From the first time I heard her say these words, it helped open my eyes to what an act of courage it is to say, "I want things to be healthier and easier for this child I love."

Allowing your child the opportunity of early intervention gives an advantage that previous generations desperately needed but were not aware of at that point in time. It was never offered to me to have anyone to talk to, and man, did I have more than several sessions' worth of content. But it was a different time as a teen in the '90s, and while my struggles were massive, they did not carry some of the complexities that teenagers of today are facing.

Which leads us to our next truth, and something that surfaces in my office several times a week, if not daily.

Truth: sometimes, when adults try so hard to be seen as relatable to kids, they become unrelatable.

When teenagers are told by adults, "You know, I was a kid once too," the message falls far short of the intention and is met with stereotypical rolled eyes. Because the reality is that, yes, we all had to deal with adolescent insecurity, awkward social situations, difficult peer relationships, parental rules, and the stress that comes with school. However, from approximately Gen Z and beyond, there are additional layers of stress for them that accompany the existence of both the internet and—drumroll—social media.

For instance, the number of times that young people are asked to exchange nude photos in any given day far surpasses the number of times they can even keep track of. From my understanding, it is brutal out there, and so many times, female clients will tell me that they are simply tired of saying no, so they cave.

The combination of the world at their fingertips and a not completely developed frontal lobe often has disastrous consequences. Once, a thirteen-year-old had a meltdown in my office because her phone died, and she had been waiting for a Snap from some random boy at school. I reminded her that she only had twenty minutes before she could connect to a power source again, and yet she sobbed that there were screenshots she *needed* to show me before the following Wednesday, or she would just fall apart.

Yes, I am happy to report that she did, in fact, make it, but not without a level of angst that kids of the '80s did not have to contend with. Sure, waiting in general is hard, but the dynamic of having so many ways to feel insecure at any given time did not exist in the same way. I've empathized with teenagers about breakups, because it was different before social media. One didn't have to witness their ex moving on rapidly, with a new profile picture and photographic evidence of the new chapter beginning. Kids can see their peers making a TikTok without them and become fully convinced it was an intentional slight. They can see a YouTube of someone explaining how they, the content creator, have a certain rare mental health diagnosis, and the viewer can become convinced that they, too, are afflicted with the very same thing.

Today, being left on "read" can send a teenager into a tailspin, having a streak intentionally broken can mean a relationship is over, partially swiping can communicate lack of concern, and having an incredibly high Snapscore is the ultimate flex. No idea what I am even talking about?

The relief on teens' faces is always palpable when it registers that I understand what they are talking about in any of these areas. Does this mean that sometimes I will have to go home and do more research on what a particular word even means? Indeed. While I never am disingenuous about what I know and will readily admit if I do not know a viral video/song/whatever, there are so many repeated trends that it does not take too long for things to surface in my office that are part of teen culture.

Like generations before, adults are often out of the loop when it comes to what terms are current, and the music and interests of kids are often dismissed. Knowing Taylor Swift lyrics, in my professional opinion, has been more effective than several of my grad school classes in helping kids feel seen. "So, it sounds like he kept you like a secret and you kept him like an oath?" I heard myself say the other day, for example. A resounding "Yes!" was all the response I needed to learn that an effective strategy is not to act like one has lived as a local in their world but to try to be an engaged tourist.

The phrase that could assist in shifting the dynamic is "Help me understand." Let me be the learner, and you tell me what I don't get. For the truth is, we *don't* really get it. Knowing that so many of my young clients are obsessed with Minecraft doesn't mean that I relate to spending hours creating something that could be destroyed in Survival Mode. However, understanding all the related terms, including playing in Creative Mode (which would be more my speed, for the record) and having the sand tray toys to boot, makes such a difference in helping a kid open up. They can tell me that someone in their life is presenting like Enderman or The Wither, and that helps give language to the anxiety they are experiencing. Again, that is why I went to grad school, to teach myself one day about zombie pigmen and *Five Nights at Freddy's* (which I *very much* do not approve of, thank you for asking).

What I have seen, though, is that kids, when they witness that you care enough to be in their world, open the doors wider to give you access to the areas where they could use some extra support.

Truth: none of us, at any age, will ever fully share until we feel completely emotionally safe to do so.

Did I want to tell someone safe so, so bad about my Utah experience without clothes, food, or water? Desperately. Did I believe that my mom could handle hearing about the depravity that happened? Not a chance in the world.

To far less of an extreme, kids tell me how there is something they want to share with a parent, about issues ranging from sexual identity to a seemingly benign preference to mental health, but they know that it would change the very dynamic of the relationship with the parent, so they withhold. I have heard so many times about one wanting to reveal pieces of information about themselves . . . as soon as they move out.

The reasons run far and wide, ranging from "My mom will say something like, 'And yes, that is why I am the *worst mom ever*'" to "My dad will just say that it is my fault I am in this situation, so suck it up."

It is easy to be dismissive when we feel defensive, for sure. But I wonder what it would look like if there was a system where our kids could approach us with a no-penalty zone of sorts and where honesty was encouraged above all else. Connection is the goal, and it is far less likely to happen without having relative safety in easier conversations.

Truth: our kids won't come to us with the big things if we act ambivalent to the seemingly small ones.

Look, I get it—there are so many words flooding out of mouths all the time, every day, from every direction, and sometimes it is just sensory overload. My friends will say, "How many listens did you have today?" and it makes me laugh, because the math of it all sounds like a lot. Because it is. Being talked to all day, I become even more thankful that my golden retriever, Willow, cannot verbalize her every thought. Her puppy dog eyes are quite enough, thank you.

However, I believe that my willingness to hold space to listen to what might land as a small-to-medium story (girl drama, video game frustrations, locker room spats, unfair school assignments, technology fails, etc.) sets the stage for the harder things to come. Why would someone open up about abuse if in the unspoken relationship test between us, I was unable to be fully present about their basic interests?

Kids are wondering, "Do you care about me as a whole?" One of my long-standing teen clients once wondered out loud if I would still like her if her parents weren't paying me. I assured her, without divulging how complicated being an insurance provider is these days (separate conversation altogether), that it is indeed not the finances keeping me in the game. The point was to validate her—*I choose* who comes in my doors, and I am actively saying yes to sessions with her out of choice, not obligation. However, my client's inquiry really touches at the core of what I hear kids/teens/young adults ask over and over in various ways:

*Am I...
okay?
worthy?
enough?
loveable?
good inside?*

Truth: many feel *irreparably damaged* from things done *to* them, often starting in childhood.

In my initial intake with parents, it is important to me to stress the importance of framing counseling as a gift, rather than something being wrong with their kid. "Can you imagine what life would be like had we had a safe place to sort things out when we were ten?" I remark. Parents typically rapidly nod and guffaw about how life would have been *a lot* better.

There have been quite a few clients who have come my way who have had a mother wound in terms of abandonment. While there is a more common story of a single mother raising a child, it sometimes happens that the role is reversed. There is something primal about having a maternal abandonment story, and at the end of all the talk/art/play, the theme often remains with the client feeling as if there is something inherently wrong with them as a human to have an absent mom.

Naturally, the tendency is to exclaim, "Of course it is not your fault! It is about mental illness/drugs/money/narcissism/addictions! It has nothing to do with you, and it is *all* them."

Yet try metabolizing that reality at seven, twelve, or fifteen and not making it about yourself. Magical thinking is a term often used in conjunction with child development. The egocentric idea of believing that one has more control over their world than they do is one that we may grow out of, but some of our thinking patterns have woven their way into our identity and firmly planted themselves.

So much of my work with abandoned/traumatized/wounded kids centers around the idea that there is *nothing actually wrong with them*.

To be congruent as both a human and a clinician, the work of my life is to put inner elbow grease into unpacking that discovery. We are not typically taught this emotional depth, and it is, in my opinion, crucial work in becoming wholly ourselves.

Helping younger generations feel deeply grounded within starts with modeling behaviors, and that starts with us owning where *we* were once wounded. The reality is that it is not just the stories of overt abuse and neglect that need healing. All of us who were once eleven, all of us have had interactions with other humans on this planet who did not always treat us the way we deserved. We have all been shamed, hurt, lied to, betrayed, and taken for granted. We all have patterns of behavior, insecurities, pain, worries, and ways of living that don't always serve us well. That is the price of being human, and the tax is our hesitation to do the work. However, when we intentionally shift even one area of our life into a healthier direction, it offers up room for those around us to be freer too. And the freer we are, the safer the world becomes not only for us but for the generations that follow.

#truthbombs

6

#barbiewasntwrong
EQUALITY MESSAGES MATTER

You're going to start getting sad and mushy and complicated.
—Weird Barbie

AS PERHAPS A SURPRISE TO many, one of the motion picture hits of 2023 was *Barbie* which was *not* aimed toward the six-year-old little girls of the world. Truly, the movie was an incredibly well-done feminist manifesto, calling out so many accurately misogynistic ways in which the world operates. In my favorite scene, Barbie and Ken enter the Real World, and instantly Ken is a big fan. It's not a surprise that Barbie feels deeply uncomfortable. "There's no undertone of violence," Ken says.

"I very much sense an undertone of violence," Barbie replies, deadpan.

Barbie, played by Margot Robbie, was actually picking up on the relentless current that is often in the air, unseen but certainly felt, and often referred to as the male gaze. According to feminist theory, the male gaze is a sexualized way of portraying women. It depicts the female body and personality as an object for men to view, own, and conquer.

To be clear, this section is in no way intended to be a male-bashing or accusatory chapter. It's quite the opposite. Due to the reality that there are many wonderful, amazing men, it begs the question of *what is going well* in our education of boys, so that we can harness that existing wisdom. There are safe men in my life for whom I am grateful, and they make up pieces of a template of what it means to bring healing and positive masculine energy into the world. My friend Steve has helped parts of me heal by being a *consistently safe* man in our Refuge community. While I am naturally cautious of men from the start, Steve has an approach that is disarming, and he is a great example of a trustworthy guy. He shared in a group setting that he had first been intimidated by me but tried to build a friendship via my dog Zoe. It worked. Over time, I watched him show up as an amazing partner to my friend Nanette, a solid support to her four kids, a problem solver ad nauseam, and a really fantastic Refuge teammate. My nervous system relaxes when he is around, for which I am grateful. And Willow, my new puppy, is completely obsessed with him and his beard, so. . .

My honorary brother, Chuck, is one of the best pediatric nurses and fathers and is an overall good human. He once facilitated at our House of Refuge event, and the rules were that only the women could talk. He wanted to hear from all of us what it was like to be a female in this world, and it was the men's job to listen. In case you are curious, there was not any awkward silence that night. Men (and women) can offer corrective experiences to one another, which is an act that helps someone heal from past encounters, in a way that is transformative.

When a child has a dad, for example, who rages when something is spilled or broken, it can naturally cause one to cower when something inevitably happens in those categories. Say down the line there is a stepdad who recognizes accidents are a part of life and reacts with compassion; that interaction can help heal some of the wounds left behind.

In a published article on the *Barbie* movie, Anna Gephart writes, "Most women do not need to know what the patriarchy has done to them, we already know. What we need is for men to listen to what we are saying and see the damage that has been done, not only to women, but to men, too."[10]

The engaged dialogue many were having about themes depicted in the movie (normative societal patriarchy, unrealistic expectations for women, self-acceptance, and body love) clearly was part of the intention. This dialogue became prevalent in numerous sessions in my office following the release. In fact, that is what brought me to see the movie, as teenage girls were reporting to me deep and insightful connections and intense realizations after getting all dressed up in pink and sparkles, expecting a lighthearted film.

Camryn, sixteen, revealed to me after seeing the movie that she had experienced elements of a sexual assault at her recent homecoming dance and felt silenced by her peers. This is an all-too-familiar story, but Camryn took courage from a scene in the movie, likely the most memorable of them all. The most powerful monologue in the *Barbie* movie comes from the character Gloria, played by America Ferrera. Unleashing all her thoughts in trying to explain to this doll who has come to life what it is like to be female in this world, she says,

It is literally impossible to be a woman. You have to be thin, but not too thin. And you can never say you want to be thin. You have to say you want to be healthy, but you also have to be thin. You have to have money, but you can't ask for money, because that's crass. You have to be a boss, but you can't be mean. You have to lead, but you can't squash other people's ideas.

You have to answer for men's bad behavior, which is insane, but if you point that out, you're accused of complaining. You're supposed to stay pretty for men, but not too pretty that you tempt them too much or that you threaten other women because you're supposed to be a part of the sisterhood. But always stand out and always be grateful. But never forget the system is rigged. You have to never get old, never be rude, never show off, never be selfish, never show fear, never get out of line. It's too hard! I'm just so tired of watching myself and every other woman tie herself into knots so people will like us. And if all of that is also true for a doll just representing women, then I don't even know.[11]

This dilemma plays out in lives, our teens' lives.

My client was afraid to tell her parents, as the boy was already heavily bragging about his evening. She shared that there was a new derogatory nickname being shared around school based on the location of the encounter. For her, it was easier to say that she was willing than face the wrath of how her peers would respond if she came forward telling the truth. Because she rationalized her part as fault in the story, there was so much residual guilt. Yes, she knew he had a reputation; yes, she had been drinking; yes, she did wear a revealing dress; yes, she allowed herself to be in a room alone with him. And yet.

This is where we have an opportunity for a more informed job communicating that *consent is everything*. Circling back to the point of how listening to mundane details paves the way for the hardest conversations is crucial. In my experience, when concerned adults hear things related to the topic of sex, the ability to be a good listener can be compromised, and all bets are off. **We need to stop blaming and shaming the victims of violence for not knowing, doing, or saying enough.** The silence is perpetuating a repeated cycle in our world, and the rape crisis centers are not becoming any less full.

In the show *Black Mirror*, which is essentially *The Twilight Zone* with modern-day technology, there is an episode where everyone wears a camera and must speak consent into someone else's before engaging in sexual behavior. While the show is satire, the principle seems to make a lot of sense.

Being sexually assaulted is one of the deepest violations that can happen to a woman. It messes with sense of self, body image, agency, intimacy, and sense of justice. To that end, girls and young women who have been harmed in this way develop a distorted view of sex and come to see that the world as a little less safe than it was the day before. For me, when I started owning the truth of my story, the constant flashbacks felt endless. The classic images of trying to scrub myself clean in the shower were reflective of my inner reality. My brain was haunted by image after image of my worth being literally poked, prodded, and evaluated, and my value measured by what my eleven-year-old body could provide to a man. The casualties of this war against women (and men who are survivors too) are bottomless.

Now, while there is no excuse for the depravity I endured, one must wonder about the messages that this population of men received about women as small children. Were they taught to protect females, use their power wisely and appropriately, and to read body language as a tool for empathy?

Uh, no.

Which makes me want to communicate to everyone with young boys in their life: Please, please tell them that they have power, innate power to change the course of history by being more sensitive, more aware, more awake with the reality that they can help make the world safer. Yes, females can be abusers too, no question. Everyone needs to get the empathy memo, yet sometimes we let the boys leave the classroom at this lesson. Why is that? Because this is an uncomfortable topic and, as a rule, we like our sense of comfort.

At my old kickboxing studio, two other women and I were talking at the end of class with our lovely male instructor, Cristian. It was almost nine p.m., so I was already prepared to head to the parking lot with my self-defense kitty kat key chain between my knuckles. Cristian noticed and asked, "Why would you need that?" The other females and I blinked at each other, and after an extended pause I responded, "Um, you have never been a woman walking alone at night in a dark parking lot, I take it?" (No, no, he had not been.)

Truly, it is a privilege that Cristian, and many others, often male identifying, do not have some of the common concerns associated with being female. These include, but are not limited to, don't live on the first floor of an apartment building, always walk with someone else when it is dark, don't leave your drink unattended, don't give your address away too soon, check your backseat before you enter your car, lace your keys between your fingers at night, don't dress in a way to invite unwanted attention, etc.

In a group this summer, a friend asked me about my goals related to kickboxing. My instant response was, "I want to look like someone a man would think twice about before attacking." And I mean it. My desire to feel safe in the world is an inside job, but the package on the outside can most definitely contribute to security.

In the past decade or less, we have done an increasingly better job empowering our younger girls, teenagers, and young adults through marketing. There *is* an undertone of violence in this world. And it sells so many things, from items related to protection and security all the way to products in the world of fashion and cosmetic surgery. Thus far, it has worked consistently for me. Not only do I have the aforementioned kitty knuckles, but my self-defense stash also includes the Birdie (a loud alarm), a Swiss army knife, a Taser gun, and pepper spray. And yet I still do not feel safe on a consistent basis. From listening to countless young girls and women over the years, neither do many of them.

We need to continue to be aware of our friends, our kids, and our family members who fight the demons of trauma daily. When I hear of another person, either celebrity or local, losing their battle from PTSD/anxiety/depression, it grieves me. However, it always makes sense. What we need to create are future generations who do not need to escape the tyranny of this world but have the tools necessary to take on the demons that are killing our children.

The key is to have a level of awareness that supersedes all the bullshit being thrown our way—and to fight back against it, with boys learning how to be allies at a young age, alongside girls stepping into their sense of power, alongside everyone doing their part to see each other clearly.

Here is a launching pad of some actual communication that could help young ears and would be so good for all of us to incorporate into our vocabulary:

You're allowed to take up space.
You don't need to be agreeable to be acceptable.
Your needs matter.
You deserve to be taken care of.
You can always try again tomorrow.
You are easy to love.
Your opinions matter.
You are capable of handling this challenge.
You are not alone.
You are a human who is worthy of feeling.

You don't have to be happy all the time.
Your complicated feelings are allowed here too.
You are never too much and always enough.

No doubt that hearing some of these messages early on could change the trajectory of kids' self-image development. If a person, from early on, receives the message they are easy to love, it is possible they may feel a bit more inoculated from unhealthy teenage relationships trying to convince them otherwise. Or if a child is told they don't have to be happy all the time, they may be less susceptible to marketing strategies trying to sell quick fixes to find (perceived) bliss in their adult lives. In order to combat marketing indoctrination in our society, we need to see more clearly how we are being convinced to buy more products in order to feel better about ourselves and become more whole. Instead, we need to start at the root of it all: the language we are giving our children to defend themselves, feel internally resourced, and equipped to support one another.

As a little girl reading books with princesses or Barbies in distress, I never resonated with the idea of a prince rescuing me from a castle. (Also, don't kiss me when I am in a comatose state, please and thank you.) Our little boys also do not need to be given the message they are expected to be the rescuers. We need our kids to have inner confidence so unshakable that anything resembling manipulation or unfair branding is immediately discarded.

And as Weird Barbie, my personal favorite, played by Kate McKinnon, stated, "We're all getting played with, babe." It's time for us to drastically change the game. Let's give them all wisdom and fortitude to be their own champions.

#barbiewasntwrong

7

#retreatingwithin

DISSOCIATION IS A TRIP

> *Parts are just little inner beings who are trying their best to keep you safe.*
> —Richard Schwartz, *No Bad Parts*

IN 1989, BEFORE WE REALIZED it was a horrible idea to have a ten-year-old testify in a live courtroom, I, while on a booster seat, sat on the stand to publicly accuse my uncle in person of child molestation. My uncle (by marriage) ended up pleading guilty, yet his lawyer was still determined to find some sort of loophole in this process. I will never forget how the defense attorney asked me, "So . . . Stacy . . . I hear that you are quite the advanced little reader, yes? . . . Would you say that . . . sometimes you live in a fantasy land?"

I was ten—not clueless (thank you very much)—and I had read enough *Encyclopedia Brown* to know where he was headed, so I simply tilted my head and said, "Um, no, sir."

That was enough of that.

Later that afternoon, my mom declared, "Well, since you are a woman now, let's go get your ears pierced!" (Perhaps she might not be up for any posthumous parenting awards?) And that is how faux emerald earrings accompanied my return to Mrs. Stivers's fifth grade class, who was told my extended absence was due to (drumroll) mononucleosis. You're all welcome, former peers, for getting to research that term so they could "learn" why I had been gone for so long. Because honesty.

Again, it was the '80s. We didn't have trauma-informed care, awareness, body safety conversations, or a game plan about how to show up for kids returning from the scene of an uncomfortable secret crisis. Because the truth is, no one knows exactly how to support the parts of a person, albeit a child, that we cannot see or experience ourselves.

When I was fully covered in ants from playing unknowingly on their hill as a preschooler in day care (oh, I remember), they knew how to respond. At the same after-school care in third grade (who I assume had good insurance), I broke my right arm playing King of the Mountain (I lost), and the workers knew how to scoop me up and take the next steps to get me to the hospital.

However, finding out that a little girl has been sexually molested for seven years, despite her pleas for help, doesn't come with a policies and procedures manual. To this day, my ability to ask for help is one of my least developed skills. To be met with outrage in the face of desperation leaves an impact, and the work of my adult life is to defeat some of those limiting beliefs in the way of seeking support.

For me, the silence made me turn inward. Since my outer world was full of chaos, I did the only thing I knew how to do: protect the sacred space that literally could not be touched. While the actual point the defense attorney was trying to make was incorrect, that it was somehow a story from a book that I was making my own, the truth is that while being aware of what was being done to my body, I abandoned it for a better, cleaner, safer world of my own creation.

Using dissociation as a tool for survival is not a premeditated act of preparing for impact. Dissociation is the way the

Dissociation Is a Trip

mind copes with too much stress, such as during a traumatic event. Defined, *dissociation* is a complicated sense of disconnection from the world around you. It's a break in how the mind handles information, thoughts, feelings, memories, and surroundings. For many survivors, dissociation is a natural response to trauma that can't be controlled.

To survive the abuse of my childhood, I personally created a super-secret cave, where no one could ever hurt me. My truth that has felt sacred for my entire life is now one that perhaps could provide insight into the world of a traumatized child. Alone feels like the only guaranteed safe place, until proven otherwise.

My world in my mind was my sanctuary, the only place no one could touch me—on any level. It felt to me I was so clever, that, sure, you might have access to my body, where I have no say, but you don't make the rules when it comes to my mind. One of my favorite books as a little girl was *Matilda* by Roald Dahl, where she outwits her abusive parents, using her intelligence to survive and ultimately overcome. Ms. Honey, her teacher, became her safe haven and a figure I looked for at every turn in childhood.

When I was sent to Utah, my precious cave became extra advanced, as the abuse and torture were much more intense, requiring more elaborate rooms to hide. To that end, I created a basement in the cave—the part of me that could not be accessed and I retreated far, far, below the surface of the earth. It was my own sacred space—separate from the harm and allowing me to stay somewhat intact.

The problem with these types of survival mechanisms, however, is that they outlive their usefulness. What is at one time the only option to stay mentally sound also paradoxically prevents the good from entering once the coast is clear in the future.

It has always been the saving grace of my life that my mind was completely untouchable. But it is very much like the proverbial gilded cage, with a lack of freedom and a false sense of security. As an adult in the healing process of deep trauma, my mind can instantly resort to falling right down the stairs of the cave when triggered, or flashing back to a memory, and also subsequently dissociating in that scene. It's complex, but the challenge is to help people be honest about what they are experiencing in order to get thrown a ladder to emerge.

In my experience, what has been helpful to me is to be completely honest, regardless of how shame filled it may feel. This kind of honesty opens up new possibilities. As Brené Brown is often quoted as saying, "If we can share our story with someone who responds with empathy and understanding, shame can't survive."[12] Many survivors, especially kids, do not want to admit that they are no longer in reality at moments, because of the general lack of misunderstanding of dissociation. No one wants to be perceived as "crazy."

For those supporting someone with trauma, my encouragement would be to experiment with what helps a child open up, as just asking might not net a great deal. And to that end, also figure out what *not* to do. When I hear an adult using baby talk with a child, it makes me physically recoil. In Montevista Hospital when I was ten, a therapist came to talk to me about my sexual abuse disclosure. She knelt down and said, "Let's talk about the mean man who hurt your 'feelers.'" Yeah, Nadine, we are not getting anywhere, I will tell you that right now. Fun fact: the only two female therapists were both named Nadine, so ten-year-old me wondered if that was a prerequisite to be a clinician. Pretty sure it is not.

Work with trial and error and see what fits best as you try on various supportive costumes. If a child with a physically traumatic past freezes on the baseball field in practice, for example, a conversation afterward would be beneficial. "When this happens, what do you think would *not* be helpful? I am also willing to do whatever it takes even if I look ridiculous if it helps you thrive."

Typically, the lighthearted nature of the conversation can pave the way for a more meaningful one. It is likely that there is a far less intense solution to dissociation for the baseball example, but the fact remains that each child/teen/adult with trauma is built so different. For some in that scenario, it might be a welcome relief to have a parent take them off the field for a breather and a snack. For other kids, they would rather sink into the soil before that would help. It's a complete act of love to find what works. Ten-year-old Isla shared that when she feels overwhelmed, she creates a rocket ship in her mind and "blasts away." One step removed from the intensity, she feels safer, which ultimately helps her regulate her nervous system on her terms.

I will have families use code words for things that help snap the child/teen back to reality, depending on how far gone he or she is into their mind. For many, hearing a random word like *fluffernutter* can suddenly change the channel. Then the tools we've talked about regarding sensory grounding and tapping into our five senses are now able to be accessed and utilized, as they are literally in the part of their brain that controls logic and reason.

On December 30, 2021, a community close to my office in Superior, Colorado, experienced a beyond-devastating wildfire. The Marshall fire killed two and became the most destructive fire in Colorado history in terms of buildings destroyed. Joining an organization of local therapists offering to provide pro bono counseling to victims of the fire, my caseload soon included people impacted by the tragedy. There were 1,084 homes, and one of my teenage clients' homes was included in that statistic. Naturally, there was a considerable amount of PTSD after fleeing from the fire, and Kellie, fourteen, struggled with things related to memories of that day.

Feeling sad at a friend's sleepover months later, when Kellie's friends (whose homes in different neighborhoods survived) wanted to make s'mores in a backyard bonfire, she completely checked out. Normalizing the reality of this trigger isn't the only step, but an important one. The next move is to share ways that she can preemptively make choices that best suit what would benefit her psyche.

Now, does one want to be left out of their friends' fun? Of course not. Moving forward, it is important to empower her with how to find the language to push back in future situations. This includes recognizing some of those internal warning feelings and allowing it to be okay not to join in on everything. Because teenage girls don't always have a keen sense of awareness of what that bonfire might bring up for their friend, they can't be expected to inherently know. However, it is never too early to help kids start to practice empathy in action, and awareness is the path there.

Practicing dialogue in times when the pressure isn't on is key, so that the words become so familiarized it feels natural. My close friends know that scary movies and books are out for me, in addition to anything that has the hint of false imprisonment or sexual violence. Since I have been clear for a long time about these categories, it flows without thought. However, when unexpected triggers surface, I also must practice healthy communication in asking for support. Someone will want to tell me the plot of something that has an ominous title, and I will interrupt—"Um, before you go on, is there sexual violence in this story?"—as my triggers are mine and might not default to land on their radar. It is empowering to kids when we allow them to own what they are willing to tolerate and would also prefer to take a hard pass on.

Haylee, sixteen, left a toxic relationship with a boy who happens to play on one of her school's athletic teams. Being anywhere near him is activating for her, as there were elements of fear in their dynamic. She feels clear that at least for now she is not interested in attending any of the games with her friends, as we talked about the cost-to-benefit ratio. The bottom line is that it is not worth it to be deeply uncomfortable for the sake of image, as there are plenty of other social opportunities available.

For me, extra acts of taking back control of something that has the potential to be highly triggering are a step toward integration and further away from being sucked into a world where I don't want to be. Checking in to what we want to be present for helps us from checking out, which is out of our control.

Personally, I believe the uptick in teens diagnosing themselves with DID, dissociative identity disorder, is a reflection of this concept—an internal created world, even a chaotic one, feels safer than the world they find themselves in. (I mean, to be fair, have you seen this world lately?) Most teenagers representing this diagnosis tell me that they first heard about it on TikTok from a relatable person suggesting certain signs, such as if you have ever lost track of time, you might also have DID.

Truly, from my side of the couch, it has been frequent and consistent: adolescents are convinced that a perceived trauma has occurred and fractured their mind into different personalities. Now, while DID is a rare diagnosis—typically not experienced unless there is *severe* trauma—there is validity in the idea of splitting off parts of our ourselves to make things make more sense and feel more palatable. Do I think the frequency with which kids are surfacing with this diagnosis is clinically accurate? No. Do I think it is worth examining why they feel the need to fracture parts of themselves to show up in the world? Absolutely. I consider whether it is more enjoyable for them to create this rich inner world because of the high level of conflict at home/school/extracurriculars. Are they bored, perhaps having an existential crisis of sorts, and needing to create a world that has a perceived purpose and meaning? Perhaps.

Seventeen-year-old Leighton came to me with depression and anxiety and a self-diagnosed label of DID. My experience of Leighton was that when there was a topic she was uncomfortable with, she retreated into a "different" personality, with no recollection of where she was or what our conversation was about. This dynamic is tricky, as no one, including this clinician, wants to call someone else out for perhaps being slightly disingenuous.

How I manage this complicated scenario in my office is to approach from the lens of Internal Family Systems. IFS is a type of therapy that believes we are all made up of several parts, or subpersonalities. When I was learning about IFS, I realized I had a part of me that I called Dobby, from Harry Potter, that was meek and willing to do anything not to get hit. Realizing that as an adult, I can choose not to enter relationships with an unsafe dynamic; that "part" of me is no longer very prominent, but is still a facet of who I am.

In my practice, I validate the "part" of my client showing up, and I realize that for whatever reason, it feels safer to that human to bring forth this piece of themselves to share. To some extent, we all do this to varying degrees. We all shut down around certain types of people, and we all show up in ways that can be different with people we are closer to.

We all dissociate at times. Whether it is spacing out in a moment to driving home and not fully recalling the whole journey to daydreaming about some event in the future, we all check out sometimes. When it has come to the level of dissociation to cope from trauma, however, therapists must determine, as helpers, how to best show up in a way that is as unique as the person in front of us. Ultimately, we need to continue to make our world a more desirable one than the one our kids, teens, and young adults feel the need to escape *from.*

#retreatingwithin

8

#waitforit
CONTROL ISSUES

We could no longer accept the things we couldn't change and decided to change the things we couldn't accept.
—Kathy Escobar, *Turning Over Tables*

REGARDLESS OF HOW MUCH WE want parts of our stories to have happened differently, or even not at all, no amount of will, wishing, or wanting can make it come true. Trust me, I've tried. And I have listened to countless amounts of people who are desperate for circumstances beyond their control to change.

When I worked in community mental health, my department was the Adolescent Intensive Outpatient unit, and we primarily saw severely suicidal teenagers. It was as challenging as it sounds, but I grew so much as a clinician and remain grateful for that season. The modality of behavioral treatment used as the only protocol was dialectical behavior therapy, also known as DBT. DBT is a modified type of cognitive behavioral therapy (CBT) and is all about skills training, which is centered in four areas, one of which is distress tolerance.

Today was an incredibly challenging day, and seeing as I had an entire caseload full of clients who absolutely deserved my full presence, the option was to draw from my internal reservoir of distress tolerance skills. Dialectical behavior therapy became a daily part of my language in my community mental health days, so the information was readily available. Since it is my policy to try always to practice what I preach, my habit is to use skills before they are taught by me in a clinical setting.

Gearing up for the day, my intention was to lean into the skill called "riding the wave." The technique involves accepting and surfing the emotional intensity, rather than trying to suppress or avoid them. Instead of fighting the wave, recognizing that the feelings won't last forever, we lean into it. The reality is that there is an ending. The brain cannot withhold the level of challenging emotions for an extended period without relief, even if that respite is brief.

Throughout my day, various opportunities for distress tolerance skills showed up, one after the other. Oakley, thirteen, shared this morning through tears the angst about a traveling situation to that would be happening that weekend. After finding the best moment to jump in, I described and talked about the skill called "radical acceptance," which at its core is accepting reality at face value.

The goal is to help practice sitting with what *is* and to prevent pain from turning into suffering. My coaching to Oakley was to focus on how she can regulate her body during this upcoming trip and to really home in on what was in her actual control. Oakley's mom texted me later, knowing I couldn't tell her the details of our session, asking for her own advice on how to support her daughter this weekend. My guidance was to use language about controlling the things she can control, remembering that everything else she might stress over is wasted energy.

All of us can use this practice more often, present company included.

In the beginning of the school year, for example, students often have many complaints about the teachers, the classes, the people in their classes, the time of day of said classes, the content, the assignments, etc. Of course, venting about our day to day is a staple of standard communication, healthy to do with your safe people. However, when the issues lead to rumination—repetitive thinking or dwelling on negative thoughts and their causes and consequences—it becomes a contributing factor in depression and anxiety. For me, the grief of the reality of my story is currently hitting me in a new way as this book is being formed, and integration is, as Glennon Doyle would say, "brutiful."

———

Today, intentionally practicing radical acceptance mantras in the bathroom in between each of my eight clients partially looked like realizing the following:

I cannot control the fact that an entire year of school simply did not happen in my formative years, and sometimes it makes me feel irritatingly curious about how much knowledge is lacking due to that gap. I *can* now control how much learning and reading and growing takes place in my world. *I am in charge of my growth.*

I cannot control the reality that my innocence was brutally stolen from me. I *can* control the influence I have on so many young souls, to help make their childhood a far better experience than mine. *I can control my impact on the next generations.*

I cannot control my reality as an orphan, having lived without biological family my entire adult life. I *can* control my willingness to accept love and support from chosen family now. *I can remember to be open to help and feeling cared for.*

Control Issues

I cannot control flashbacks. I *can* control my choice to talk about them with my therapist and trusted people, not masking how damaging they are to the quality of life. *I am allowed to tell my story without a filter to my safe people.*

I cannot control that the neglect and abandonment in my early years have created within me deficits, namely resorting to retreating deep within when I am in pain. I *can* control my determination not to turn a blind eye to the suffering around me. *I can hold others' pain.*

The cold hard truth is that no one can "fix" someone else. It is just not possible. In addition, every time a parent tells me that they want me to "fix their kid," I gently remind them that their child is not broken.

The fix-my-kid request gets under my skin, because the implication is that a person is not operating according to the user manual. The last time I checked, there wasn't a manual. There is no right way to person, and while there are societal norms and personal values, we are so much more than that. No one can tell me what they would do in my situation, because they are simply not me. And truth be told, I would not want a single person I love to live a day in my shoes. Not for all the money in the world, and to that end, we need to realize that we can't control another's circumstances.

From what I have seen, it appears we want to control circumstances that are simply beyond our abilities and to also change other people. Several times a day, I hear myself say, "Since we can't control what another person does, how would you personally make choices different in this situation?"

This afternoon, one of my sweet and sensitive eight-year-old clients was talking about a scary villain in Fortnite and wanted me to look it up on my phone. (*Super* excited to see what the algorithm gods do with that one, but that is despite the point.) He was creepy, not going to lie, but then we went back to doing sand tray therapy. At some point, he looked up at me and said, "I am really sorry if you get nightmares because of Siren Head."

While assuring him I would be fine, I omitted the fact that my dreams come directly from the hell I endured, and video games have no power in infiltrating the landscape that operates my current level of reality. To that end, I promptly ordered the figurine when he left for him to bury/attack next week in the sand, as an extra layer of assurance to him that my mental health is not impacted by said villain.

How much easier would things be if we had the power that kids possess while yielding the game controller? Minecraft, Fortnite, Roblox, and Animal Crossing are the main ones I hear about daily, and it is always interesting to ask kids about their favorite games, as this can be really telling.

In the Roblox universe, for instance, there is a bottomless pit of options available, and kids get to build and literally create anything they want. What would it be like if our lives were as The Sims are and you just followed simple instructions and manifested exactly with the right formula? While I believe that we make so many choices that create the life we want, unforeseen roadblocks and challenges—and, let's face it, life in general—gets in the way and interrupts our illusion that we are in absolute control.

Later today, another teenager was sobbing about wanting to be an adult already and not feeling respected because she is underage. After validating that it is hard to be a teenager and that she has less power and less freedom, I offered a gentle reminder that there is literally *nothing* she can do to advance her age on a timeline. And that accepting that she will not be a minor her whole life, and that her current reality is not her forever reality, is crucial to her current mental well-being. Radical acceptance for the win!

Control Issues

Several weeks ago, my dear friend Katie and I took a long weekend trip to the Hot Springs in Nathrop, Colorado. It was an incredible experience and otherworldly to be in steaming natural water as snow was falling. We met other friendly women also on a girls' trip in one of the hot tubs, and we started chatting with them for a while. When one lady asked my job, I hesitated, as this can be a party foul, but answered honestly with a laugh. Katie and I now exchange a look when we travel and encounter these kinds of situations, and she knows to not disclose my profession until I do. Not always the wisest move to share one is a therapist with strangers, just saying. One of the ladies responded with, "Oh, how has your job changed since COVID?" Since my body temperature was already pretty warm, I knew it would not be a long conversation because I'd have to exit the pool soon, but I basically said that we all saw anxiety spike through the roof, and we became aware as a society how fragile some things can be. However, we also saw so much resilience and the ability to adapt to a changing and unpredictable environment.

Her friend responded, "Wow. You must be so tired." Well, yes, friendly stranger, I *am*, but not from supporting, listening, and offering presence. My weariness comes from my own personal burdens and wishing that I could make all the pain vanish. My exhaustion comes from fighting things beyond my control and trying to push the monsters down under the bed, when they no longer are willing to be contained. "I mean, a little," I shrugged instead.

In recovery circles, the Serenity Prayer is a staple for centering meetings and always recited at gatherings: "God, grant me the serenity to accept the things I cannot change, the courage to change the things I can, and the wisdom to know the difference."

We can learn a lot from those in active recovery, and knowing the difference does appear to be the battle. My soul, kids' souls, and every other person's soul all need to be reminded that their lives are worth it. Sometimes the fight admittedly gets to be so much—and I am constantly encouraging kids it gets better. But we need to show them with transparency that there is life beyond struggle. While it is crucial to me to practice appropriate self-disclosure, as I have been on the receiving end as a client of the opposite, sometimes kids need to hear from me that it is possible to emerge from crappy circumstances.

Someone asked me this week if I ever get really, really sad, and my first thought was to call one of my close friends on speaker and let them answer for me. I blinked before saying, "Absolutely. You know why? Because I am a human, and it is part of the package deal."

While my presentation may sometimes be shiny and available, it is more important to be seen as human. My self-leadership coach, Jordan, observed last week that I often appear as a golden retriever, not showing when I am hurt or in need. While appropriateness is key, as adults, sharing our humanity with the younger generation is valid, healthy, and ultimately beneficial.

In the musical *Hamilton*, specifically in the song "Wait for It," Aaron Burr sings about his deep determination to find his time to shine despite Hamilton's steady rise to power. It's a constant reminder that we are the author of our story. We may not have had any say in the beginning chapters, but we can control the narrative from here on out.

Despite the trauma we have been through, the challenges, the injustice, the struggles, the mental illnesses, the heaviness of being a human in this world, the reminder is clear: you are worth it. Our kids, our families, our friends, our clients are all in our lives not by chance but for a higher purpose. My belief is that it *somehow* all matters, and even though we may not have much clue this side of death, all parts of our story help create a glorious tapestry that will one day make much more sense.

It is up to us to be the one thing in life we can control. #waitforit

9

#empathytraining

HOW TO HELP

> *"I don't need anyone" is a statement often made by those who at some point needed someone, but no one showed up.*
> —Sara Kuburic, It's On Me

LIVING FOREVER RENT-FREE IN MY head resides one very specific, very powerful performance from *Six the Musical*. *Six* is a musical comedy with a modern retelling of the lives of the six wives of Henry VIII of England during the sixteenth century, presented in the form of a modern pop concert. In the show, each of the wives takes her turn singing her story to ultimately determine who suffered most from their common husband.

Catherine Howard, the fifth wife at age seventeen to King Henry's forty-nine, weaves her story of being groomed at a young age and being used for her body over and over and over again. In fact, one of her first lines is "And ever since I was a *child*, I'd make the boys go *wild*." Um.

History tells us that she was in fact abused, assaulted, and taken advantage of by numerous men throughout her young life, which ended at approximately age nineteen. The incredible actress who originated the role on Broadway portrays such a powerful version of the song "All You Wanna Do" that her account has now become my most favorite song from a musical, hands down.

The original interpretation of the song gave the appropriate emotional intensity to the words, so that the actual reality of what she shared isn't lost in the intentionally upbeat rhythm of the performance.

The actress sadly and then also fiercely croons, "All you wanna do is touch me, when will enough be enough?" which truly serves as a battle cry of aching and mistreated young women everywhere. Saying that her rendition makes me personally feel both seen and heard is an understatement.

How many times are females (especially) revictimized due to not being protected or believed? Important to note that abuse is not gendered; however, statistically speaking, people who are female identifying have a much higher rate of victimization across the board.

King Henry allegedly found out, among other things, the "sexual past of her childhood" and handled it by having her immediately beheaded for the crime of adultery. It is also reported that Catherine Howard claimed among those instances that she was raped, and the fact that she was initially touched at age thirteen (and probably younger, let's be honest) lends itself to the reality that regardless of any detail, she was, in fact, a victim.

Deeply tragic, and yet still somehow sadly and incredibly relatable in modern times. So often in my practice, young teenage girls share with me how they have been sexually violated but feel as if it is their fault somehow for a variety of reasons, ranging from consuming alcohol to sending too many messages on Snapchat to not saying "no" loud enough. To add insult to injury, some of these girls have meekly attempted to communicate with someone else, the "safe adult" that the pamphlets tell them to, only to be denied their dignity and shamed into abject silence.

Thirteen-year-old Kayla was brought to me completely distraught and full of so much visible shame. It took her a while to be able to look into my eyes, and when she finally did, she sobbed for a good portion of the session. Kayla was a victim of a sexual predator on the internet, an adult who posed as a child on one of the extremely common online games. She finally was able to relay the story, and as it turns out, she was slowly groomed, as textbook as it gets.

When she fully realized what was happening, she felt predictably trapped and unable to find a way out without revealing what she felt was her responsibility in the scenario. She had already been coerced into sending nude photographs and then was on the hook for doing so, as her predator had clearly intentionally planned. Our work was untangling her ownership in the victimization from the reality that a grown man preyed on a child in a very strategic way.

While it would make sense for a parent to feel a variety of emotions connected to the discovery of this situation, my desire would be for us to try to lean more strongly into the reality of how scary and confusing that must have been to *be* Kayla, while also holding the truth that the *secrecy* was a breeding ground for the petri dish of abuse.

Now, it is considered a felony for a child/teen to have a nude photograph of even *themselves* on their own device. Therefore, if a situation like Kayla's happens, prosecution is often not sought after by the victim due to the reality that Kayla, too, would be facing a child pornography charge by having her own pics in her possession. In our state of Colorado, she would herself then be labeled as a sex offender on her record.

And yes, kids these days are warned over and over about the dangers of social media and technology and strangers. They also don't have fully developed frontal lobes, so critical thinking is typically not a strong point, and situations like these are sadly not uncommon. Jonathan Haidt states in his book *The Anxious Generation*, "The two big mistakes we've made: overprotecting children in the real world (where they need to learn from vast amounts of direct experience) and under protecting them online (where they are particularly vulnerable during puberty)."[13] However, when things happen, (because have you met kids?), they will need safe places to land and hope to not face compounded shame once a revelation is made known.

We need to be safe enough people for others to want to bravely seek support.

As I've shared earlier, one of my own deepest core memories is also one of my earliest, in which I was sexually abused at age three by an uncle. The scene in which the abuse took place is vivid, for sure, but the one that haunts me was my mom's response. I can picture everything about the scene, quite literally, which is the gift and curse of an often photographic memory. A summer Sunday in Las Vegas, at my grandma's house, sitting on the shag carpet by the recliner at my mom's feet while she was clipping coupons from the newspaper. I finally got the courage to tell her that my uncle, her brother-in-law, had touched me in my private area, and my mom, in no uncertain terms, flipped out.

Yet, in an extremely misguided way, her rage was *at* me. Screaming, accusing, and hysterics followed, and I cried loudly but held on to my truth. My grandma came in from the kitchen and was quietly saying, "Terry, you should listen to her." My mom said, "If that is true, she can stand up and tell the whole family!" and continued screaming and fuming.

Since my mom was just too distraught, I quietly made my way to the bedroom and played by myself (with encyclopedias—I was a weird kid) until she calmed down, and I subsequently "forgot" about the exchange. My uncle, completely unaware of the previous day's explosive conversation, promptly "babysat" me the very next day. My mom, a single parent, used his help as she worked as a dental hygienist throughout the week. She played racquetball that weekend with my abuser, while I watched through the glass doors at the gym. The arrangement did not skip a beat despite the accusations, as of course they had fallen on deaf ears.

A former therapist found it fascinating that I remember thinking to myself as a child, *One day she is going to know and feel so bad for this.* I had pictured her on a cloud, looking down, reviewing her life, and realizing *too late* how wrong she was.

My mom would much later—on the day I testified in court—reveal her deeply buried demons that prevented her from being able to show up fully for me, or really at all. As a preteen, a traumatic incident happened to her, and perhaps an empathic move would be to tell the details in the court parking lot? Horrible timing, but hearing her story, and knowing that she had never told another soul about the brutality that happened, likely helped contribute to my future as a therapist.

It wasn't until I was ten, and hospitalized for depression, that I was able to communicate about my own sexual abuse that had now been taking place for over seven years. Let it be noted that my shared information was in a questionnaire I filled out, and that was all that it took for me to be heard. Someone asking. In paperwork. In 1989. That was all. Just asking outright if someone had touched me.

I figured that the Montevista Hospital staff would know what to do and I was safe in a locked facility. Also noteworthy is thankfulness that we handle kids in much more sensitive and child-centered ways in 2025. However, I will always remember the kindness of a male worker who, upon learning that he shared the same name as my uncle, intentionally took off his name tag when he interacted with me. Can I also advocate here for the correct anatomical terms to be used when teaching kids about the body? My family (surprise!) did not, and it proved to be difficult to describe what happened to me, using words that sounded like cartoon dialogue.

I also recall in third grade, sitting crisscross applesauce on the gymnasium floor, when we had an assembly about "stranger danger." The speakers made sure to remind their audience that if someone was hurting us, go talk to a safe adult. Eight-year-old me was basically mentally smoking a cigarette, dramatically putting out the ashes, and smirking, *Safe adult? Please. Find me one.*

By then, it was too late for me to believe that my teacher who taught me cursive could convince my mom, and I sure as hell was not going to have a repeat scenario of the original confession. Thankfully, two years later my stepdad joined the scene, and he was able to observe that even though he didn't know much about kids, this particular one seemed much sadder than fifth graders typically were in the '80s. It is because of him that my story changed forever. Because he was paying attention. His awareness changed the course of things, and while my childhood was, well, awful, his insight made it possible for my uncle to be convicted as a sex offender.

The fact that my mother turned a blind eye and then subsequently had me sent away a year later to Utah to "help me heal," in which the most unfathomable abuse happened, is a partial plot line for so many of our vulnerable young people. Not knowing how to respond and then making it even worse can happen if we do not hold an attuned level of consciousness.

Studies show that the response to someone revealing for the first time an abuse that occurred can have a deeper emotional impact than the incident itself. If a revelation is met with comfort, belief, and reassurance, it can help people develop a reservoir of inner healing that creates a neural pathway leading to a felt sense of support.

My journey did not develop that way, and one of the hopes of this book is that at least one person can be heard by a safe adult asking the right questions and making it possible for healing, even if the story is painful to hear. One adult having a hunch after reading any of these pages and listening to what their gut has been saying, then asking a child direct questions about their safety will make it all worthwhile. Because I had sealed lips about what was happening to me, because it made more sense just to endure it, my thought was that the touching that was happening to me was my fault. Please: make it incredibly clear to the kids and teens in your life that nothing is ever too big, too confusing, or too much to be able to navigate *with* them.

After my mom died, twenty-three years ago, my stepdad casually mentioned, as we were preparing her death certificate, how horrible she felt about her lack of parenting abilities in my childhood the rest of her life. Since I only started talking about the nightmare in Utah about a decade ago, she went to her grave never knowing the magnitude of the abuse. As an only child, it is deeply painful for me to hold both the awareness that she was poorly misinformed about how to parent as well as the knowledge about her fighting her own inner battles. While it feels like a bit of a betrayal to her memory to write about now, the intention remains to shed light on an area that could be prevented for another family, in another time, in a similar scenario. That also feels worth it to me.

While my story is on the more extreme end, different pieces of the variables can actually add to the same equation. Research shows that being sexually assaulted puts you at higher risk of being assaulted in the future, and experiencing childhood abuse or domestic violence also increases the chances of future victimization.

When someone survives sexual assault or rape more than once, people are more likely to think there is something wrong with the survivor than with the perpetrator, which is the definition of victim blaming. The men who abused me as a child when I was captive also mentally and verbally assaulted me with cruel language intended to accuse me of being damaged as a person and therefore susceptible to sexual behavior.

The message of it being my fault was deeply ingrained into my young psyche and has taken decades to sift out, with residual guck finding its way to the surface on occasion. The belief that we have been irreparably damaged would be my one wish for every abuse survivor to have eradicated from their souls. In my decades of listening to hard and difficult stories, this common thread is so intensely weaved into the abuse narrative that without it, people would suffer so, so much less.

John O'Donohue said, "There is a place in you where you have never been wounded, where there is a sureness in you, where there's a seamlessness in you, and where there is a confidence and tranquility in you."[14]

To this day, rather than ask for help when I am emotionally struggling with memories, I often tuck into myself and hide. And I have language and the ability to communicate the reality swirling around. Sometimes, the darkness feels too dark to navigate, and the dense floor to get to the nearest person feels too thick.

Here's the new truth I can lean on: I have amazing, incredible, available people in my life to seek support from. Even despite this reality, my tendency is to retreat deeply within. However, always striving toward growth and healing, eventually my turtle head pops out of the shell and seeks to choose healthy behaviors. How much more is this tendency to hide common for those who cannot identify others who will empathize with what they are going through?

Vulnerability is the way to freedom, and having lived this experience both personally and professionally, I can attest to the truthfulness of the virtue.

As Brené Brown states, "Vulnerability is the key to connection and the path to the feelings of worthiness. When we shut ourselves off from vulnerability, we distance ourselves from the experiences that bring purpose and meaning to our lives."[15]

Empathy, as defined in the *Merriam-Webster Dictionary*, is "the action of understanding, being aware of, being sensitive to, and vicariously experiencing the feelings, thoughts, and experience of another." Going one step further, one could add that *understanding* another's pain is definitely not the same as assuming we know what it is like to have lived through their story.

Do I think that you need to have been through trauma yourself to have compassion for someone who has? Absolutely not. In fact, some of my closest friends who know the real depths of my story do not relate whatsoever to the chaos that was my childhood.

And I am thankful for that.

Recently, on the cover of *People* magazine, Mariska Hargitay was featured with the bold title "I'm Stronger Than

I Have Ever Been." For twenty-five years on *Law & Order: Special Victims Unit*, Hargitay has played Olivia Benson, a police detective who strives to bring justice to survivors of sexual violence. Off camera, her advocacy work created Joyful Heart Foundation to "help survivors of abuse and sexual violence heal."

In interviews, Mariska has started sharing for the first time about a sexual assault that happened to her three decades ago. She explained the relief she felt after sharing her writing.

"I think it's a matter of physics, right?" she said. "If we hold a weight, it's very heavy. But if it's sand and we all hold a piece of it and we carry it for each other in our society, it's not as heavy. So for me, naming it was really powerful, and I feel lighter. And it was time not to carry that."

Unable to process what she went through, Hargitay said that she "cut it out" and "removed it from my narrative." But decades later, she's standing in her truth. "I now have so much empathy for the part of me that made that choice because that part got me through it," she said. "*It never happened.* Now I honor that part: I did what I had to do to survive."[16]

One of my seventh-grade clients, Hayden, attempted to die by suicide last week. She told me, "I have been trying to cry for help, asking to see you more, and saying over and over that I am not okay. They finally heard me." Thankfully, she did not realize that a very small handful of pills was not a very effective strategy to be successful for her fatal endeavor, but absolutely did accomplish her communication goals to get an emergency therapy session.

At her appointment with me, Hayden confessed that she still did not feel like she could keep herself safe. Bringing her dad into the room and telling him that his daughter did, in fact, need to be hospitalized is not the best part of my job, that is for sure. Her dad blinked at me and said, "But . . . why is she so sad?" Honestly, it was a fair and real question from a parent baffled about what he is hearing and wanting to make sense of it all.

A huge misconception, happening every day, is that the outside projection of how someone shows up in the world equates to serenity and happiness on the inside. Incredibly confusing regarding some individuals, including famous celebrities whose personas clearly did not mirror the dark realities they were facing internally.

This is where psychoeducation about depression and anxiety can prove to be extremely helpful in the face of both the confusing world of teenagers and life growing up in this current reality. Often, I see parents take the blame for circumstances that are far out of their reach or control. At least once a month, parents are reminded that it is typically never the people who are "worried about ruining their child who are actually ruining their child."

Also, let me repeat that every child I know of is being raised by humans, and that package comes with an extreme margin of error. The hope is that we continue to do even better than the generation before, with better education and more awareness. Below are some tips that are conversation starters and ways to show you want to be a person of support.

I am here for you.

I got you.

Truth is, I have no idea what to say, but I am on your side.

I am here to listen without interrupting you.

Is there something you would tell me if you didn't think you would get in trouble?

You really can't convince me that you aren't a good kid/person inside.

If you had one wish about what I would understand about you, what would it be?

How to Help

What is challenging about being you right now?
Do you want me just to be with you right now?
Tell me what I may have missed hearing you say.
There is nothing you could say that could make me love/support/care for you less.
Even if I don't understand, I want to learn.
How can I help you in this moment?
I am sorry for not hearing you sooner. I am here now. Please let me try again.
What do I seem not to get about you?
If you could redo a conversation we had, what would go differently?
Do you want my advice, or do you just want to be listened to?
We'll figure it out together. (my personal favorite)

My self-leadership coach, Jordan, often says, "I'm in your corner," which makes me smile every time.

While I realize that some of these sound suspiciously therapeutic, I, in fact, am a therapist, so I come by it honestly. And this is what kids need more of in their lives, not only in their therapist's office. My desire is that some of these serve as a launching pad into further conversations that deepen the connection between us and people we love and want to support. Our kids/teens/adults are hungry for understanding and the relief that comes from being truly known and loved anyway.

Catherine Howard, for one, deserved far more championing than she ever received in her unreasonably short lifetime. As she woefully sings the final chorus, the actress's whole body literally shakes with accuracy that anyone who has ever been violated can attest to. The passion in which she belts, "Why did I think he'd be different, but it is never *ever* different?" poses a real challenge to us in the twenty-first century.[17]

Let's continue to create better endings and to hold vigil for those who have never been and never will be heard. Let's stop saying, "Why didn't you say something sooner?" and instead proclaim gratitude they now feel safe enough to report. Let's stop judging people who have "a pattern of behavior" and get curious about what has happened in the landscape of their backstory. Our kids, our clients, our friends, our families, and our people all deserve a voice. For simply the reality that they are alive, they deserve a witness. While Catherine Howard in the sixteenth century will never receive true poetic justice, albeit almost five hundred years later, gifted actresses will make sure, through an integrated portrayal, that she is *finally* both seen and heard.

It takes incredible bravery to face the memories, chapters, moments that haunt us—no question, I know for me it is my highest value to cherish the relationships I am in, so I continue to do the work, show up, heal, and I continue to tell my story.

Let's help others tell theirs too.

#empathytraining

10

#andalso
HOLDING CONCURRENT REALITIES

Are people born wicked? Or do they have wickedness thrust upon them?
—Glinda the Good Witch, *Wicked*

"THE POISON YOU FEEL INSIDE you," my therapist, Melissa, softly said, as she stared directly into my soul during our last session, "is not coming from *inside* the house. Sometimes people break into our houses, and they leave poison on the countertop. The poison does not belong to us, and we do not need to keep it. The poison that you feel inside does not belong to you. You have seen the darkness; you are not the darkness." I blinked at her. Twice, in fact.

An understatement, indeed, to say that this specific conversation *fundamentally* shifted my perspective on the healing journey. Conceptually picturing the actual removal of the dark as originating from the self was an extremely effective exercise, and the metaphor remains solid in my mind. The separation of *what is done to us* from *who we truly are* feels at the very crux of the issues of the soul. So many young people who have been somehow abused or neglected begin to have thoughts about feeling tainted or partially defective for the first time and bravely share with me reasons why they feel different. I hear it all the time as a clinician, even from friends, and feel the reality of it myself—that if people only knew, they wouldn't see me the same.

For so long, I have deeply struggled with the idea that if the greater world beyond my intimate circles knew the full extent of my backstory, it would potentially render me unreliable as a solid clinician. However, as an invested therapist advocating for kids/teens/young adults to live out the truth of who they are, emotional congruence is much easier said than done. My dear friend Nikki Kennedy, who is an incredible trauma therapist, shared with me that the honesty of a clinician would make her personally *more* likely to seek out their support. My takeaway from that conversation was that being real lands with more significance, even if it isn't very pretty, than presenting a self that is less than fully integrated.

As Brené Brown states, "The definition of vulnerability is uncertainty, risk, and emotional exposure. But vulnerability is not weakness; it's our most accurate measure of courage."[18] I realize that if I am to model healthy behavior as a clinician for younger generations, then it is the work of my life to continue to fuse my story into the woven tapestry.

A related concept that I often teach my clients, typically in the range of tweens and up, is what I like to call the "and also" strategy. Important to note, we can inadvertently invalidate people if we are to offer a response to their pain with a "Well, yeah, *but* you have this going for you/at least/others don't have," etc. The heart behind this "and also" technique is a gentler approach in terms of balance, as opposed to "Yeah, but . . ." The addition of the word *also*, when it comes from the sharer themselves, is an opportunity to observe what *else* is true about their current reality.

Lately, the concept of the idea of dialectics—the truth that two opposing things can be true at once—has been occupying my brain space. As aforementioned, I once worked at a community mental health center, hired for the Adolescent Intensive Outpatient unit. The protocol for counseling, and in fact the only approach we were directed to take, was to handle sessions using DBT, dialectical behavioral therapy, mentioned in #waitforit. DBT is designed to address and teach emotion regulation, distress tolerance, mindfulness, and interpersonal effectiveness. DBT, in a nutshell, has the clinician accept and validate the client's feelings while also informing them that some of the behaviors are maladaptive. One of the strategies in sessions with severely depressed teens that my supervisor strongly encouraged is called a paradoxical intervention. The intention behind this approach is to challenge the thought, feeling, or behavior in such a way that ultimately helps them see that they have the power to change a symptom.

Memorably, one of the teenage clients at the agency assigned to me remains significant years later in my continued professional development. As a therapeutic relationship, it was the one that both challenged and also stretched me the most as a clinician. Hadley, sixteen, was severely depressed, heavy into self-harm, despised everything about school, claimed to hate all people, and had extremely challenging home dynamics. Hadley had gotten very attached to a therapist in the program who suddenly quit, which, as you can imagine, did not in any way positively impact the client's mental health.

Our program was intense, as stated in the name, and had required weekly components of two days of three-hour group therapy sessions, one session of individual therapy, and one session of family therapy. We saw these kids quite a bit, as they were all high need, actively suicidal, and deserving of a great deal of support.

I worked with Hadley for quite some time after her previous therapist left, which, regardless of the reasons for the departure, cut deep into her abandonment wounds. One Tuesday evening in the middle of her session, she started screaming at the top of her lungs at me that I didn't even care about her and wanted her to be dead. Had this been the first time she had this same tirade, it would have jarred me a little more. After working with her for countless hours and pouring everything into trying to help sustain her, I decided to attempt the paradoxical intervention that my supervisor had been encouraging me to do.

Hadley, inches away from my face in my office with warm light, said I probably went home wishing on stars that she would just kill herself. I looked at her calmly and said, "I call bullshit." We both looked at each other stunned for a moment.

"Um, what did you just say?" she asked.

"I call bullshit. If you didn't think we cared about you, you would not show up here four times a week voluntarily, you wouldn't have shared with me important parts of your story, you wouldn't ask to see me more than you already do. It is bullshit, Hadley. Now let's talk about what you really *do* feel."

There was a moment of silence before Hadley burst into tears and admitted that she was terrified about losing me too. Now we're talking about something real. When she was able to admit that she still ached for her old therapist, and that it wasn't a violation to also feel connected to a new one, healing and actual growth could take place in the therapeutic relationship.

While that relational intensity rarely reaches the walls of my private practice, that story has stayed with me and is an example of the coexistence of so many layers we hold. Someone told me today how they felt jealous but still relieved about a situation they had been in, and we processed how

Holding Concurrent Realities

sometimes emotions really manifest like a rubber band ball of so many colors. In *Inside Out*, when Sadness begins touching the memories and Joy is losing her mind (tee-hee) about them not being solidly happy core memories, the #andalso message came through loud and clear. Similar to the mottos within the recovery community, we are learning to deal with life on life's terms.

In my office, teenage breakups come up quite often. While walking kids through the process of feeling their hurt, it is also crucial to let them know the emotions do not have to be all consuming. Often, I will say, "Yes, and what is our takeaway? What do we know now that makes us a better person and wiser in future relationships?" One of my clients recently said, "I have learned that it matters how he treats my friends." So we are hurting because we feel like we were just discarded, *and also* . . . we gained valuable insight that we can carry with us on our next chapter. In no way does it negate the pain we feel, and the ache will dull, but now we know what we will never ever put up with in the future. #andalso

So much of the time, we want to save our kids and friends from ever experiencing pain, so jumping fast to the lily pad of "You are better off!" can be a good launching point but isn't enough to help propel them forward in an empowered way. Shaming a child saying that "kids are starving in Africa, eat your dinner" does not actually help anyone, but rather enforces the internal belief that somehow they won a cosmic contest, yet someone deserves it more. Do we want to teach our kids gratitude and empathy? Without a shadow of a doubt. Are there ways to do so without adding a heaping of ineffective guilt to the mix? Absolutely.

When something tragic happens in the world, we often find the famous quote from the iconic Mr. Rogers surfacing. "Look for the helpers. You will always find people who are helping." My purple tank top with this message is one of my favorites. I'm always reminded that despite the horrors we read about and endure, there is so much good being done in the world, at all times. #andalso

Black Mirror, as mentioned earlier, a modern-day version of *The Twilight Zone*, is set in a near future dystopia. Each of the episodes is stand-alone, so you can watch each one (or stop watching one) independent of the others. The thread among most of them, however, is that there is some kind of technological advancement that goes terribly wrong. One that often replays in my head is an episode called "The Entire History of You." People can flash a playback of any memory onto a screen to share with others. Every moment of one's life is recorded and can be shown to prove things, to get opinions, to clarify something, and to provide evidence. As you can imagine, and as is with most of this show's episodes, it doesn't end well, and there is a catch in how the perks improve living in society.

Thinking of this episode, and despite the dark social commentary *Black Mirror* is trying to make, I find myself wishing we had at least some ability to record the nuances that happen in our lives. As a clinician, it seems like family therapy scenarios could translate a lot more clearly if we could see with our own eyes what happened with that huge conflict about screen time or the Thanksgiving debacle that continues to resurface every other year.

My hunch is that sessions would spend a lot less time debating the facts and a lot more talking about the unmet emotional needs. However, the people viewing the story may all have differing perspectives anyway, but he said/she said conversations could be brought to a halt. My non-therapist friends often remark how challenging and/or intense the subjects must be for me to listen to all day long. While there

Holding Concurrent Realities

is some truth to that, I would rather talk about things that matter—even if they are dark and scary.

Exactly one month ago today, my thirteen-year-old beloved and seemingly healthy golden retriever, Zoe, unexpectedly tragically died on a Friday night. She was as active as ever when I left in the late morning, happily jumping up into my backseat before I headed to a Refuge Lake Day (our anticipated all-community summer event at Boulder Reservoir). I was pulling people on tubing boats all day long, and while it was exhausting, it was, as always, an incredibly fun time. I came back home to a dog who was seriously debilitated and unable to walk.

Zoe ended up needing to be put down about an excruciating hour later and died peacefully in my arms. Not leaving the house for three days straight, crying nonstop, I scoured the internet specifically looking for a golden retriever puppy. I had known that the next dog coming to live with me would be trained to be my therapy dog. While I thought it would take some time to find the right one, it was not too long until I laid eyes on my future furry companion.

The stars aligned—in a seriously beautiful turn of events that left me with no doubt that she was the one. Willow, my new baby golden retriever puppy, has helped heal my heart in the aftermath of the ache of Zoe's sudden death. In her going on three weeks with me, she has been adopted as the mascot for both my cherished faith community, The Refuge, as well as my happy place—my kickboxing studio. She has been a fixture in my office, and she has been snuggled with, posted about in clients' Snapchat selfies and in my own Instagram stories, cried on while sprawled on laps; she has doubled as a weighted blanket, been a bridge for a reluctant client on the spectrum, given affection to kids who believe themselves to be unlovable, created countless smiles and squeals of joy, and loved on strangers literally everywhere we go.

Prior to retrieving her (pun intended), I slowly shared with clients the upcoming shift in my office. People were delighted, but many parents would tilt their heads and say, "But what about Zoe?" So, one by one, they learned Zoe had died. While incredibly sad and devastating, at the same time the intention was to show capacity for another little love. An opportunity to discuss how two drastically opposite feelings are not mutually exclusive. Furthermore, even with the dark feelings and various levels of struggle for anyone, the light is always still there, however dim. In fact, my most favorite quote from Victor Hugo, straight from *Les Miz* expressing this sentiment, is on display in both of my offices: "Even the darkest night will end, the sun will rise."

In the darkest of moments, my own frustration simmers deep within concerning the life I have been given. And yet? I am *also* deeply proud of who I have become. When the icebreaker in group settings comes loaded with the question, "What is one word you would use to describe yourself?" my go-to choice for years has always been *resilient*. My ability to bounce back has been actively cultivated by the act of doing my own healing work. However, the cost of developing resiliency is an incredibly high one. And also? The ability to tap into an internal reserve of deep empathy does not develop from a smooth and unbothered path.

Glennon Doyle writes about this relating to children and what it means to watch kids begin to struggle. She writes, "More than anything, I want my kids to grow to be brave, kind, wise, resilient humans. So what is it in a human life that creates bravery, kindness, wisdom, and resilience? The bravest people I know are those who've walked through the fire and come out on the other side. Maybe our job as parents is not to protect our kids from pain, but to hold their hands and walk into pain with them."[19]

The truth is that life is literally always full of the hard and the beautiful, the terrifying and the exhilarating. And our kids will learn these truths throughout the journey of their lives, but having the little conversations over time about paradox and acknowledging things are rarely *all good* or *all bad* can lessen the shock of when life inevitably happens. Objectively, it empowers us to look within at our internal resources before looking outward. It is the difference between saying it is too much and saying that the hurdle is in fact big, but there is nothing one cannot conquer without support.

Rainer Maria Rilke states it in the most beautiful way regarding the infinite paradox: "Let everything happen to you. Beauty and terror. Just keep going. No feeling is final."

#andalso

11

#strongheartsclub
THE GRIEF PILGRIMAGE

Someone did us all a grave injustice by implying that mourning has a distinct beginning, middle, and end. That's the stuff of short fiction. That's not real life.
—Hope Edelman, *Motherless Daughters*

TODAY HAPPENS TO BE JUNE 9, which coincidentally is the twenty-third anniversary of the very day my mom took her last breath. When I was fifteen years old, my stepdad sat me down on our burgundy floral couch and told me my mom had been diagnosed with breast cancer. She had been given six months to live, per the oncologist. Also, she was about to have tricky surgery on her spine, because the cancer had spread through her bones, and we might be building a wheelchair ramp attached to the house because there was a chance she would be paralyzed because of it.

Thankfully, she was not in fact paralyzed. In actuality, my mom ended up living almost seven more medically tumultuous years and was on experimental medication when she died. She did, however, end up having in total seventeen surgeries, and doctors performed a mastectomy in 1995 on the wrong breast. True story. Years later, in college when I shattered my ankle ice skating, the doctors had me write "yes" in Sharpie on my right ankle before my surgery, as documentation of the accurate limb. Couldn't help but wonder how many incidences proceeded that protocol to render it necessary. My thoughts going under were obviously about my mom, and I woke up with a ton of metal in the correct ankle, so well done, doctors.

When I was in high school, my mom was in and out of the hospital more often than I could count. Performing in school theater and being also very active on the speech and debate team, my hospital visits included coming with a full face of stage makeup. Not crying, aware that with so much caked on my face, it would be obvious if I did. That strategy contributed to the frantic stuffing of dark emotions to be later unpacked in therapy as an adult.

I would leave cast parties and forensics tournaments early without a word, silently slipping into a medical portal where my stubborn independence festered and became the norm. At sixteen I truly felt lost about who to talk to, and mostly no one in my life knew what was happening at home. Mrs. Litterini, my favorite teacher and forensics coach, the safest adult in my life, was always a secure haven at school. And even then, the language to describe to her the angst within eluded me. No one knew how hard it was to come home to an empty house because both parents were at the hospital, or to watch her decline when she sporadically returned home. Let alone the dark shame I carried like an ever-present invisible cloak. Keeping incredibly busy, doing all the things, and smiling at all the right times has made me keenly aware of my clients with the same tendencies.

Had there been an attentive therapist to confide in, my journey would have undoubtedly been so much less painful. An opportunity to be heard, seen, and validated for how tragic anticipatory grief created havoc in a family of three? Yes, please. To talk about how confusing it was to me what was happening to my mom? What was the point of her life, then, to die so young? To have me? And if the only reason she lived was to have me, what did that mean for the pressure as to what I was to do with mine? What does this mean cosmically? Being raised in an agnostic home made me wonder if anyone or anything bigger was even paying attention.

While there were no satisfying answers to the questions swirling around my brain as a teenager, the relief of being able to say some of those things out loud to an empathic party could have made such a difference. Just a theory.

Grieving children and teenagers have unanswerable questions that we cannot fully satisfy. However, making them feel less alone in the confusion and validating those existential questions can be the missing piece in nervous system regulation. If someone had looked at me and said, "What is it like to be you right now?" I cannot even begin to tell you how that could have changed the trajectory of the emotional turbulence of my teenage years.

My mom died eleven days after her forty-ninth birthday, a month after I had just turned twenty-two. No one my age I knew at the time could relate, as much as they tried. People would tell me stories about how they got in a recent fight with their mom, or how some gerbil had once died, or how someone they knew had an uncle whose mother died of cancer. One of my Starbucks managers (where I worked in college) said that looking at me made him sad, which *I think* was an (awful) attempt at sympathy? Perhaps? The line so often verbalized was, "I can't imagine how I would go on if my mom died." Telling you right now, that was helpful to me exactly zero percent of the time. The intention, for the most part, was to empathize. However, for me it felt as if the speaker was now coming from an entirely different frame of reference, as this kind of response further alienates the listener within their story. It is if they are saying, "I know that you must feel so alone and confused right now. I don't know what it is like to feel alone and confused, and in no way do I want to." Yep, neither do we.

One of the challenging pieces is the reality that there is not much in terms of how to facilitate grief, beyond dealing with one-year death anniversaries. In October of 2001, Terry's Team was formed for the Phoenix Komen Race for the Cure, made up of friends, coworkers, classmates, and even professors from ASU. We won Team of the Year and Best Team Outfit (I had a picture of my mom and three-year-old me screen-printed on the shirts, which was novel back then). We raised $10,000 for breast cancer research, and at the time, it felt like I had successfully reached the boss level of the "stages of grief." Since, well, that is not even a thing, wishful thinking proved to be just that.

On the Sunday following the event, the intensity of my grief barreled into me like a bull on steroids and pinned me in bed all day long. Having nothing left to organize, channel, or distract me from the reality that my mom was no longer on Earth made me experience the excruciating truth of being a motherless daughter. Solace was found for me in the book *Motherless Daughters* by Hope Edelman, who officially coined that term. In 2001, when my mom died, Amazon was not big yet at all, but I deliberately ordered it there to reduce the likelihood of a face full of pity or an unhelpful remark from a bookstore sales associate. Now, I think it is so important to be able to speak truth, even about death, without fear of making things awkward for others. Instead, society needs to be educated about how to better cultivate environments where memories of the dead get rights to just as much airtime as the living.

Unfortunately for me, my stepdad got involved with another woman, a coworker, quickly after my mom's death. Living in another state, she and I did not have the chance to really bond. The opposite, in fact, was that I was told she wanted pictures of me taken down immediately, as I resembled my mother and it made her uncomfortable. Soon enough, the message was loud and clear that this woman wanted me deleted from the world of the only dad I had ever known, and sadly, he disappeared from my life. Had I perhaps been older, maybe I would have had more language to negotiate a relationship, yet at the same time, my counsel to teenage clients often centers around never begging for respect or love. Had she not been openly hostile about my existence, she would have known that I, all along, wanted happiness for my stepdad, and I did not blame him for wanting a relationship again, even so soon. What I wished this woman and frankly my stepdad had known was that the world is plenty big enough for us both.

Perhaps due to the dynamic with my stepdad's new girlfriend, or my mother's wishes, we did not have a funeral or any type of memorial. To this day, I firmly believe that significantly impacted my processing, delaying the acceptance of reality. It added an overall surreal sense to my perception, when grief in and of itself is already disorienting. People always ask about the appropriateness of children attending funerals, which is a fair question. Studies show when children express interest, it is best to allow participation in whatever capacity they feel comfortable.

For me, there was one hour to decide to see my mom before she was cremated. As one with a photographic memory, it was an offer declined not to have the visual in my head for the rest of my life. Like with most things, it should be left up to individual discretion—not a one-size-fits-all approach. However,

I do believe that children should be given a choice in as much as their development allows. What remains clear, however, is that children should be allowed to continue to speak about their special person for the remainder of their lives, without being subtly shamed or desperately encouraged to stop doing so. Regardless of the passage of time, the person is significant to them, and they deserve to speak their truth.

While there is a difference between ruminating and being unable to function with the pain of the past, the more likely scenario is that both an internal as well as external clock exist reminding them that the window is closing for discussion about their person. As a mental health professional, and one who will forever be impacted by the death of my mom, it is important to me that we readjust what it could look like to have conversations, even years later, about those who have died, as simply a part of the narrative of our lives.

As I was telling my dear friend Shannan once, the hardest piece remains: there is nothing truly left to *do* about grief. I mean, the candle has been lit, the Race for the Cure team has been organized, the grief groups have been facilitated, complete with sharing my story, the therapeutic crafts have been created, and the memorial posts have been published. There is literally nothing else, and while the intensity dial has been turned down over time, the hole remains. It is space to be held, not a problem to be fixed.

Well-meaning, kind people left me purple African violets on my doorstep, which was, of course, a thoughtful sentiment. However, PSA: please never buy a grieving person something to take care of without their permission. Or at the very least, if we are not confident that they are a plant person (I am so not), maybe consider another method to show support. It is so, so hard for a grieving person to find the energy even to care for themselves, to be honest. When my African violets died three days later, it was a bit of an existential crisis about the reality of death in this world. Good times.

One of the most helpful acts of love, in my opinion, is simply to take the initiative. One of the most common sentences heard from the lips of supporters is "Let me know if you need anything." The problematic part of this well-intentioned statement is that a grieving person typically has little to no energy to *ask* for what they truly need. My honorary mom, Kathy, made sure to let me know right away that she would pick up my beautiful dog Zoe's ashes and paw print for me as soon as they were finished.

We can't obviously remove the burden of grief from our people, but we *can* ask which day of the week would work to order them delivered food from their favorite place. In considering the younger populations, it might be helpful to do even the smallest things, like watching a show that you know they are into. Over the years I have worked with so many kids who are into all kinds of things, ranging from the classic Minecraft, Taylor Swift, Bluey, obscure anime shows, to even a loud YouTuber. Knowing that information from working with them, I will sometimes watch a short segment or two of a special interest subject, as a safe connection point. If I see that a kid is visibly activated in talking about grief, having a zone of interest as a detour can make all the difference. "Hey, I have a serious question for you. Who is your current favorite YouTuber?" Having a safe conversational lily pad to land on offers an easy win for distress tolerance. For the kids in our lives who are grieving, they are having to answer the same "How are you?" question more times than they can literally count. To have a safe adult have a normalized conversation about what they care about is an act of love that cannot be overstated.

The Grief Pilgrimage

A mom contacted me years ago to see her middle-school-aged daughter, Paisley. Paisley's father died of a terrible and prolonged illness, which had lasted several years. The presenting concern, however, was that her mom was dating again, and Paisley absolutely had not instantly warmed up to the new boyfriend. Ultimately—I would later learn—the intention for hiring me was to convince my future client to be open to this new male figure in her life. "Was she able to get support after the death of her father?" I had asked during the parent-only intake. Her mom said, "Well, no, but it was *over* a year ago."

My first and foremost plan was to offer space for her daughter to talk about the most significant event in her life. I recognized that the feelings simmering for her appeared to be suppressed because of the expectation to "just get past it." And in a shocking turn of events, my client *did* have a ton of unprocessed feelings relating to her dad dying before her eyes. The research, put out by the JAG Institute, a leader in the children's bereavement field, shows that unaddressed childhood grief can lead to short- and long-term difficulties, including poor academic performance, mental health issues, and early mortality. (JAG was named in memory of Judith Ann Griese, for whom Judi's House is named.) Those who had a parent die growing up said it took six or more years (without any treatment) before they could move forward. And 59 percent of adults who had a parent die growing up say they have experienced more sadness and depression in their life compared to most adults.[20]

The intention was to make space for all her feelings, which needed to happen for any new healthy attachments to form. Paisley, twelve, was full of thoughts and opinions and unanswered questions, and deserved a place in which all of those were welcomed with open arms. We created a sand art heart feelings jar, in which one picks different colors of sand to represent emotions, and the result is a layered and labeled glass container to validate all their feelings related to grief. A memory photo pillow, a decorated heart frame, and a bejeweled treasure box were all pieces of art therapy that helped Paisley to externalize her feelings, so that they no longer created suppressed disturbances within her spirit. Paisley's mom was not pleased about how this whole process was taking months. She angrily said, three sessions later, that her daughter's dirty looks toward her boyfriend were making it "uncomfortable for everyone in the room." What she didn't realize was that giving her daughter permission to not have to form an instant attachment to the new boyfriend *was* the work. Maternal anger was quickly unleashed at me for not telling Paisley to "move on" and "get with the new program." Since that type of dialogue never helps anyone, words of that nature were not part of the content of any of my sessions with Paisley.

What *was* happening—the client being seen and heard—was the crucially important missing component in her process. Just because one is not crying all day doesn't mean that they have "moved on." Grief is complicated and further compounded when another human tries to decide *for* us when we have completed the process. In addition, we had conversations about having a new man enter the environment and how to ease into that reality. We cannot expect our kids to simply delete all the previous content in their lives in an attempt to start a new chapter. While of course we want our kids to be able to move forward, we must realize that the change is not a simple one, and by trying to bypass the emotions that come with the cost of love, it just makes feelings more complicated.

A line repeated to my clients is that if we don't deal with what we bury, it rots and makes a bigger mess than before.

Children's bereavement, a specialty field, is only a few decades old, but the research has emerged to show how significant prolonged grief can be on the developing brain. The New Song Center for Grieving Children in Phoenix, Arizona, is where my compassion for children's grief became tangible, and exactly where I attribute the foundation of my career shifting. Having already graduated with a dual master's degree, I went back to school to get additional certification to specialize in children's grief. Thankfully, I was able to intern at New Song, which was one of the best professional decisions I have ever made. It was there that my wings grew and I knew deep in my bones that it was exactly where my temperament, empathy, and life experiences collided in the best way possible to be effective as a clinician. Had I known about New Song when my mom died in 2001, I would have found there a group for young adults and received much needed support. Because of this, it is always important to me to inform people of services I know about, so the word continues to get out about specialized care.

There is one therapeutic building block that remains significant and often in the forefront of my mind in helping hurting kids grieve. My supervisor, Caryn, shared that her little brother tragically drowned when she was five. When her mom took her to the first day of kindergarten, the teacher was told, "We lost her brother this summer." Caryn made sure that the language of "lost" was immediately removed from our conversations around the children, as developmentally, she was always "looking" for her brother in the hopes she could "find" him again. The grief field holds such honest dialogue—raw and real. The directive is to say "died" instead. While it may land for some as harsh, it is simply the truth. It helps not to sugarcoat or try to make others less uncomfortable (which doesn't really work anyway). "Hi, my name is Stacy, and my mom died from breast cancer." We don't say passed away, fell asleep, went to a better place—we say the facts. In addition, the phrase "special person" is used, because "loved one" might not be the most accurate term, especially if there was a complicated relationship with the one we are grieving.

What remains for me from New Song is being completely drawn to the grief world, as there is (mostly) no one to blame. When I moved to the Denver area, my volunteer work continued at Judi's House, which is another amazing nonprofit organization whose sole purpose is to support children and grieving families to feel less alone. The tenet that is a common thread in children's grief organizations is that "it is always okay to cry" and "it is always okay to laugh." Huge realizations happen for so many kids to be let off the hook and not to be expected to appear in the throes of sadness all the time. It is okay to still giggle, and it does not dishonor the reality that your special person died if one is not constantly in a hard place. It is simply the truth that one must keep living, despite the hole that has been left behind.

One of the best gifts from my time at Judi's House remains my friendship with Carolyn McDonald, a brilliant social worker. During her time on staff there, Carolyn helped form the Pathfinders curriculum, which is a ten-week guided grief journey taken by kids in each age group, in their respective developmental rooms. One of my favorite memories was during anger week, someone would get me to read the book *I Was So Mad* by Mercer Meyer to the littles, because my over-the-top animated reading was a whole thing. The truth is that it was such important work that went into crafting what would be beneficial for each of the groups to heal together. And as we know, anger is so real, regardless of age. While the younger kids would rip up phone books (because why do they make them anymore if not for this exercise), the older kids would be verbally processing the ways in which grief took something irreplaceable from their lives.

For the teen group, the week that was created to talk about "unhelpful things people have said to us" since our special person died was filled with the clichés and unintentionally insensitive things that people who do not know about grief say to people who do. This is why it is so important to listen to people who are impacted by grief (and lots of different areas of life, for that matter) to learn how to respond better, say less, and listen more. "God needed another angel," "Everything happens for a reason," and "I know how you feel" are not the best options. To this day, a phrase that I often say in my office is "I will never truly understand how you feel, as no one really knows what it is like to be you. But you will hear me say that I can connect with that idea, thought, feeling." The intention is to relate but not assume or invalidate in the process.

Over the years other opportunities to be a camp counselor at children's grief camps have given me incredible insight into what it can be like to be a grieving child or teenager. So many of the kids feel instantly connected by being part of an exclusive group that they did not ask to be a part of. The beauty of these experiences is that kids hear things they thought were secretive thoughts—out loud from another eleven-year-old in the group. Those who have had a special person die by suicide learn that someone else also feels to blame, and the kids who have had a special person die by a car accident also feel responsible for making Dad late that day. Feelings and thoughts are normalized, and that is what can happen when we are able to help kids create a safe space to tell their truths. Many times, kids/teens are the only ones in their circles who no longer have a living sibling, and the isolation compounds the intense grief they feel. To have at least one other person of a similar age share an experience can help them feel less alone in a world that has recently become more confusing and less than desirable.

One day, a big dream of mine is to open my *own* nonprofit grief center for children in the Denver area called #Strong Hearts Club. In 2013, The Refuge, my faith community, once had six kids, ages eight to fourteen, who had a parent die all around the same time. As the kids' and families' pastor, as well as a children's therapist, I was extra equipped with enough specific children's bereavement knowledge to be an adequate amount of support, so we started a monthly Strong Hearts Club. Themed around a different subject every time—including anger, stupid things people say, regret, and holidays, to name a few—the meetings gave all the kids a chance to share their feelings, and then we would do a fun activity both to get big energy out and to celebrate life together. Grief simply endures far longer than our culture allots, and it is often in the pockets of safe spaces where people can feel less alone.

As Hope Edelman writes, "I miss her when I can't remember what works best on insect bites, and when nobody else cares how rude the receptionist at the doctor's office was to me. Whether she actually would have flown in to act as baby nurse or mailed me cotton balls and calamine lotion if she were alive isn't really the issue. It's the fact that I can't ask her for those things that makes me miss her all over again."[21]

Not having a living biological mom makes Mother's Day complicated and always makes me hold special awareness for my clients who have a missing role in their lives on these kinds of days. Something to be aware of is that grief often strikes when there is no anticipation of an activating event. Of course, we can take extra care during holidays and, on their birthday or the anniversary of their death, make plans to cushion the blow. However, at my last dentist's visit, when I looked up from the chair, I felt blindsided with emotions. My memories of the fish mobile my mom had above her dental hygienist's chair made me tear up, and I was hit with intense nostalgia. My eyes teared up, and thoughts instantly went toward all the kids who are unable to articulate the emotions running through them at a similar activating moment. As an adult with incredible friends, there are safe people available to text, but even teens typically don't give themselves the same permission to initiate those conversations. Another reason it is so important to check in, as some of those moments don't land on everyone's radar. Why would they? Those grief bursts cause pain that does not need to be held alone.

Over the years, kids for whom one parent is absent have entered my office for a variety of reasons. Grieving someone who is still alive is its own beast, and clients supported through that reality struggle at a different level. It is one thing never to have the chance to make new memories; it is another to be aware that for whatever reason, your special person lives and breathes and is unable to choose you. While there are multitudes of reasons—including mental illness, incarceration, and/or addiction—the result is typically kids who deny the hurt or feel the ache deeply. Healthy therapeutic work can ease the mental noise that often accompanies an abandonment wound of this nature, but similar to grieving a death, the scar remains.

Also, can we please consider fewer events like Donuts with Dad at school or Mom's Tea Time? What about Donuts with Grown-ups? Speaking from my side of the couch, holding space for kids who are crushed to be left out of things they simply cannot manufacture is heartbreaking. Yes, often a sibling or neighbor steps in, which is beautiful—I, too, love seeing those video clips—but the cognitive damage produced in the interim is real. Being raised by a single working mom, she could not take off work for these kinds of events. Speaking from experience, this leaves children feeling a deficit that lingers. With more awareness and sensitivity, there are opportunities to plan more inclusive events that don't cause already grieving kids one more ache in their already uprooted lives.

Every time in a kids' grief group space where the leaders are also expected to share, my intention is to be appropriately honest. Typically, my response remains the same to the questions of "how you felt when your special person died": relief. Strategically, this is an important emotion to reveal, especially to kids/teens—such "taboo" emotions as "relief" are less talked about, whereas sad, angry, devastated are more likely to make the cut. Of course, those other feelings are not any less true, but there are more predictable emotions that often make the rounds far more frequently. Prolonged illness of a special person, either physical or mental, can be brutal on the heart that creates longing for closure. While my choice would be to have my mom alive, the way in which she was suffering made me feel grateful she was no longer in such agonizing pain. In addition, if there was a complicated relationship with the person who died, perhaps if they were abusive, a child/teen may honestly feel pleased or plain happy they are no longer alive. And our kids need to know that all feelings are valid, and there is no moral value to emotions.

Having personally experienced the ache of relationship loss, it reminds me how many of my teenage clients have wept openly in my office about the death of a friendship. Again, not from a comparison standpoint, but in a way that can honor that the ending of a relationship can be incredibly significant in a variety of ways. We are designed for connection, and when that is severed, the ache reverberates, and the feelings are real. Grief can happen in any relationship, and it is not limited to age. A nine-year-old does not have the skills to be able to sort through the feelings of grief alone, and holding pain to grieve someone still alive can be daunting even for adults to navigate.

And as a clinician, my tools, friends, wisdom, awareness, and years of perspective add to my ability to cope. And yet my humanity reminds me that sometimes life hurts and often in a way that nothing can *fully* soothe. Let me be clear that there is no "resolution" to grief. However, there is a reorganization of intense feelings, and one can acquire the ability to get to a place where grief is not the only one steering the ship but is still somewhere repurposed on deck.

One of the most helpful written pieces about grief was spoken once at a special child's funeral I attended and has provided me comfort over the years: "Eulogy from a Physicist" by Aaron Freeman. Over the years I have offered it up to grieving friends, and it remains one of my primary choices as a balm for aching hearts. Here is a shortened segment of the beautiful piece:

> You want a physicist to speak at your funeral. You want the physicist to talk to your grieving family about the conservation of energy, so they will understand that your energy has not died. And you'll want the physicist to explain to those who loved you that they need not have faith; indeed, they should not have faith. Let them know that they can measure, that scientists have measured precisely the conservation of energy and found it accurate, verifiable and consistent across space and time. You can hope your family will examine the evidence and satisfy themselves that the science is sound and that they'll be comforted to know your energy's still around. According to the law of

conservation of energy, not a bit of you is gone; you're just less orderly. Amen.²²

#strongheartsclub

12

#plottwist
CHANGING THE NARRATIVE

> *Friend, you are who taught me that a difficult life*
> *is not less worth living than a gentle one.*
> *Joy is just easier to carry than sorrow.*
> —Andrea Gibson

DURING THE PROCESS OF FINISHING this book, there was a significant trajectory shift in what was previously *thought* to be my intended audience, and therefore some of the main plot. In my eighteen years in private practice, the number of families entering the doors dealing with the impact of high-conflict divorce has been substantial. At this point, I've had the chance to see plenty of separated families that have had a wide range of civil and professional relationships with the other parent/parents of their children. While there are multiple reasons why their status with one another is no longer connected, everyone obviously realizes that there are still dependent children to raise. One thing I wish was true across the board, however, is that kids of divorce or separation were listened to without the loud filter disparaging the other parent and therefore being discounted.

There was an incredibly upsetting encounter with an estranged dad of teenage Samantha not too long ago that left me very clear that my time supporting kids of high-conflict divorce has come to a full and complete stop. It has become time to hand the baton of these cases to specialists who are fully immersed and highly skilled in high-conflict divorce scenarios.

We, especially children's therapists, enter this profession to help hurting kids heal and develop coping strategies that serve them through adulthood, to be a safe place in this crazy world, to offer hope in their darkest moments. To be screamed at, threatened, harassed, and insulted was bizarre to me. Because what? Especially for this particular family, my heart hoped to help their relationships become healthier than they would be without intervention. Maybe, I had previously thought, the father simply needed support with some helpful approaches and understanding of what growing up in that hostile environment felt like for his kids. Maybe psychoeducation was the missing piece of it all, and being good at puzzles, I had been more than happy to do my part in assisting where needed.

And then it dawned on me: this father, and perhaps others with a similar mind-set, are not going to be reading this book. Ever. Not only was he not interested in what I thought "winning" would be—a relationship with his daughter—he clearly saw victory in a much different light. Victory appeared to be dominance, not connection. Yet it does make me wonder if having a child pull away will help instigate a behavior shift and perhaps a search for better ways? Could that be the catalyst for change in the right direction? (One can dream.) When I was first writing this book, the prevailing thought was, if only it was articulated well enough on the kids' behalf in this kind of situation, surely it would change things for the better for the kids. Well, as with anything, one must be willing to hear the words and be prepared to do something with the feedback they have been given.

While there are millions of reasons why divorce happens, my biggest wish is that the children wouldn't suffer because of their parents' animosity toward one another. One of my teenage clients dealing with depression, Holden, has parents who, despite being divorced, meet in my waiting room for all his sessions and catch up on all things related to their only child. Holden often remarked how he realized how lucky he was to have divorced parents who not only tolerated each other but were able to stay friends, and therefore reduced the negative impact on him. I would tell him, "No, really, be super grateful. It is less common than you may even think."

Also, I want to make an important distinction. It is not realistic to swing to the extreme of being best friends with the ex, nor even advisable at the least. Because obviously, there are numerous reasons they are, in fact, an ex. But it would be beautiful to see less destructive fires being flung at one another with the child having to put them out at their own emotional expense.

In recent years, there has been a shift in legal communication about parenting strategies for separated parents: coparenting versus parallel parenting. *Coparenting* is defined as a collaborative approach for the child, including flexibility, shared ideas, and often, but not always, similar methods. *Parallel parenting* is where the parents interact with each other as little as possible, and each parent makes all the decisions about the child when he or she is in their own home. There are plenty of benefits to both styles, as the key is to reduce the repercussions for the child of parental conflict. In my observation, it feels important to be able to own the truth of the story and not set up false pretenses of a shinier picture than it really is, as that never ends up helping anyone.

One of my longtime teenage clients from an incredibly high-conflict divorce, Kaylee, plopped down on my couch not too long ago and sadly started with, "Sorry about my parents. I know they put you in the middle of the ___ issue this week. Sorry." I looked at Kaylee and said "Whoa. Let's be very clear: that is nothing *you* need to apologize for. My guess is that you are *also* exhausted about this fighting?" She widened her eyes and nodded. "Hear me when I say this: it is *never ever* the kids who are the hard part of a family's divorce. You need to know that nothing I am experiencing related to this situation has anything to do with *you* or how I feel about our work together. It.is.not.yours.to.hold."

Years ago, since there continued to be a high volume of people seeking support for their kids related to a divorce, my thought was to offer a six-week teen support group. It was posted in a wider network, so it filled up fast with willing kids wanting to talk to others who understood. Ironically, one of the groups was all tween boys signed up for those dates. Having themed every week in my created curriculum, we processed and participated in activities related to the subject matter.

During the "Changes" week, I asked the kids, "What has changed in their lives since their parents had separated?" One kid, Luke, emphatically raised his hand and exclaimed he wanted to go first. He then proceeded to pull out a cell phone from each pocket. Luke said, "Well, this phone my dad gave me and pays for, and I am not allowed to call my mom from this one or put her number in it. And this phone, my mom gave me, and I can't call my dad from it, because she doesn't want his name touching anything of hers. So I guess what has changed is that it has been confusing not to mess up too bad with the phones." Insert emoji with slits for eyes and a mouth here. Seriously.

You cannot convince me that strategy is good for Luke, serving the situation in any way, other than to further the split and animosity, for which the kids already have a felt sense of responsibility. And to be crystal clear, never have the feelings, stories, thoughts, questions from kids in my office played into my exhaustion. It is the constant battling between parents that children's therapists get caught in the middle of, therefore discouraging some colleagues from taking on that issue. Truth be told, when a children's therapist is verbally attacked, it has nothing to do with the well-being of the child and everything to do with attempting to weaponize therapy at the child's expense.

Many therapists will provide initial paperwork indicating that it is not within our wheelhouse to testify in a court of law, as doing so jeopardizes the emotional safety and confidentiality we have worked so hard to build with the child. There are other professionals who do the work of deciding who shall be awarded more parenting time, and it does not need to be the one person the child has felt safe to tell their inner thoughts and stories to. In my opinion, asking a therapist to do that undermines the whole process in the first place, and makes a child feel less safe knowing that others will hear the thoughts that have been promised to be held in a sacred space.

Look, I realize that many reading this long for peace with the other parent(s) they are parallel parenting with and that it feels simply impossible. It is highly unlikely that people with narcissistic tendencies are picking up a book written by a children's therapist, looking for a way to better support their parenting. If I felt like it would be effective, my heart longs to have real conversations with a parent who is making extraordinary emotional demands on their child, yet that doesn't end well. What I want to shout from the rooftops is "Sure, you do have the power to ban your child from things relating to the other parent, but your control is a limited-time offer." In the case of Samantha, the judge ruled that once she is sixteen years old, she can decide even whether to see him ever again. As for now, she is not required to go over and live with him another day in her life. If nothing shifts with her dad's attitude toward her as a person with her own independent thoughts and feelings, you can guess what she will choose.

All that power and money gets thrown around, when, in my opinion, hearing what his daughter was saying could have *changed the whole process* and ended far better for him. "I don't feel safe with you, your anger terrifies me, you don't listen to what I am saying" were powerful statements . . . that fell on deaf ears. Often I say to kids, "If ___ could understand just one thing about you that they do not, what do you wish it would be?" Samantha said, "I wish that he would not respond with 'Okay, Debbie," when I tell him how I feel. He thinks that I am just parroting my mother, and it makes me so angry that he doesn't realize my feelings are directly because of how he acts toward me."

It remains tragic to me that kids, who are much more profound than some adults give them credit for, are desperately trying to tell these difficult parents, who often have narcissistic tendencies, how to make their way back to relationship. The kids may get instantly dismissed by their parent, and yet one day, not too far off in the future, they will be turning eighteen. Once they are adults, they can no longer be controlled and demanded to come over despite their protests, and they will remember the experience of not being heard. The time to control is over, and if the relationship is so damaged from the process of steamrolling over their child, there is not a bargaining chip that remains. Younger people in these situations are often dismissed as repeating what they hear, but in my observation, the kids are paying attention and make their own assessments based on what their lived experiences have been up to this point.

The term *parental alienation* is also one that has been thrown around the last several decades yet is rapidly making its way out of divorce court vernacular. Often labeled as the "language of the abuser," the original goal was to accuse the other parent of "poisoning" the child against them. In reality, however, Samantha did not hesitate to connect with her father because of anything her mom was saying, but rather because of her own days living under his abusive roof. In an ideal world, parallel parenting would be seamless, and each could do what they wanted and transfer the child/children with no fanfare. Some, however, are parallel parenting with a narcissist, and it is virtually impossible to avoid conflict. From both supporting dear friends in these situations and watching this dynamic play out in my caseload, I can honestly say that the view looks awful. Sometimes, there is nothing to do but to play by the court order and minimize as much contact as possible. My belief is that in the end, the children, who again have been paying attention, will see the truth for what it is worth. The name of the game for now is survival and avoiding giving energy to the bombs that the other is constantly trying to defuse in your yard.

When I was three months old, my mom divorced my father and refused to talk about him, almost ever. She would become hostile with any questions about him, just grumbling that she had low self-estcem, and he had been nice to her. He was effectively deleted from our lives, and I only first met him when I was eighteen years old. My mom, slowly dying at that time, put his address in front of me as my graduation announcements were being labeled and said I had to send him one. We had one of the most awkward meals of my life (and probably why Olive Garden always feels just a little off putting to me).

After my mom died, curiosity got the best of me, and I inquired about where exactly he had been my whole life (a zip code away), and did he know when I broke my arm in third grade (he did not), and why did he never show up (my mom allegedly didn't allow him to be around). He died not too long after my mom, from a sudden (preventable) brain aneurysm. There was never much of an opportunity to connect in a meaningful way, once those years of childhood were no longer. Just as a reminder, there is a window of time for repair regarding absent relationships, and when it closes, the damage remains. Eighteen years, in my opinion, was past the point of no return.

When my stepdad entered my life at age ten, he showed up for me in meaningful ways. Stepparents, in my opinion, can be one of the best #plottwists around. I have seen much healing (and conflict, don't get me wrong) in the dynamic of another adult choosing to sign up for the job. Jason, a stepdad to Jayden, sixteen, has come to sessions looking for ways to better advocate for her and to help her heal past trauma. While no one anticipates having a stepparent for their child in the future, the beauty of being chosen and celebrated despite DNA is the best #plottwist.

The same can be said for adopted kids out there too. There is no denying the process and life of an adoptive family has unique challenges and complications, and also, as I reminded eight-year-old Evelyn, "Out of all the kids in the whole world, your mom and dad picked you. I know the ache is real about your birth mom, and her early death is so incredibly sad. And also? There will be unique opportunities available for you because of adoption. Your story has a new path, because your moms both said yes to giving you the best life possible." #plottwist

As Anne Lamott writes in her newest book *Somehow: Thoughts on Love*, "Sometimes it all just sucks, as Jesus says somewhere in the Gospels (although off the top of my head I can't recall chapter and verse)."[23] We often talk in my office about living out your truth in the timeline you are in. Do I wish that I'd had a decent childhood without abuse and neglect, stable parents, and a generally secure foundation to grow up from? All.the.time. And yet? The fantasizing road trip unfortunately takes us to dead-end towns with disappointing fuel stops, I am afraid.

Speaking of books, for younger me, the Choose Your Own Adventure books were among my absolute favorite reads. All different kinds of storylines, and then at some point, the reader is faced with a crossroads: "page 72 if you think Kurt should chase the dragon, or page 17 if you want him to carry on and take a safer road." While it is not typical for us to be presented with mythological creatures on our daily hiking trails, we regularly have multiple chances for our own plot twists, if we look carefully enough. Through countless life experiences, we can also help our people to see that things may not always have the ending they had anticipated. It could be better than what we ever hoped for.

One of my nineteen-year-old clients, Chloe, returned to sessions with me after she had a medical catastrophe in which she was left comatose and almost lost her life. Having seen her in her early high school days and through the COVID-19 pandemic, there was plenty of existing backstory to draw from in supporting her in this chapter. She said to me sadly the other day, "So you know how I almost died in the hospital? Lately, all these bad things keep happening to me and every time, I think, *If I had actually died back then, I wouldn't have to be experiencing* this."

"I hear you," I told her. "I do. But if we are going to go down that rabbit trail, it is only fair to say, but also, if you had died, what would be the *good* you were also missing out on? That concert that made you smile last week, that text that made you blush, that ice cream you went to get with your mom? You would also have missed out on that too. Just saying."

#plottwist

"He completely broke my heart," Peyton wailed. "I was so close to dating him, and then everything blew up." Blinking at her, I tilted my head and said, "Um, what about the reality that *he* lost the chance to date *you*? Please."

#plottwist

My entire adult life has been about unlearning the patterns that were deep set from childhood. Helping kids recognize their own behaviors and tendencies so they can save a lot of time and heartache as they age remains my passion. What if our kids were able to have safe and thought-provoking conversations with their parents about what healthy relationships look like and what signs to look out for?

Without turning into a passive-aggressive attack on the other parent, conversations could be amazing about what green flags are for people in general. Unfortunately, I will never know what my mom learned about relationships, about herself, and what she wanted for me. Based on her earned wisdom from being married and divorcing my dad, her story arc could have been at the very least interesting. What if she had told me more about herself and that knowledge in turn had helped shine a light for me in relational areas that were once dark and confusing?

#plottwist

A kid has ADHD/anxiety/depression/anger, and we worry about him constantly getting into trouble. The problems have gotten "worse" since the divorce, and what does this mean for the future? What if he had the right support, both academically and professionally, and ends up using his neurodivergence/

challenges/emotions to better our world, helping us understand how his brain works? What if our kids' obstacles at any level were not weaponized in the battles among adults?

#plottwist

What if divorce recovery in terms of the kids didn't have to be about how to walk on eggshells about the other parent? What if they could go through the gamut of emotions without being burdened with how much hostility is constantly swirling between their parents? Also noted, often there is one parent who desperately wants to cease fire, lift the white flag, and yet the shots from the ex keep coming. I see you, and your kids see you, so stay the course and know the truth will prevail. Your job is to resource your child as much as possible with ways to cope, and to also make sure there is support in place for you. There are Facebook groups dedicated to supporting one another on this journey, where others realize they are not alone in trying to parent with a challenging dynamic. My dear friend Carolyn, a social worker, always says to families, "I am going to need you to love your kids more than you hate your ex."

#plottwist

―――

My waiting room is completely decked out with a purple sloth theme, bordering on ridiculous. Those adorable creatures are my favorite, and the fact that they smile as they hold on for dear life kills me. (Deeply jealous of the fact that they only pee once a week, but whatever, nature.) Truly, they are symbols to me of faithful resilience. What if we gave our kids lessons from sloths: just hang on, conserve your energy for things that matter, focus on what is *your* problem, and simply let go of the rest.

Sandra Levins wrote a sweet children's book about divorce called *Was It the Chocolate Pudding?*[24] Two little children are dealing with their parents' divorce, and one day it tearfully comes out in a question involving an incident with food. The pudding ended up on the wall—was that the reason that everything happened? The mom reassures the children that of course not, that there were bigger issues at play. While it obviously wraps up nicely, that book has been busted out numerous times when a child confesses to me that they feel at fault for their current life circumstances and why their parents can't even be in the same room together.

While the concept of "magical thinking"—where it can feel emotionally safer for a child to blame themselves than to acknowledge that there are things at play out of their control—is a powerful contributor to this thought process, it is better to offer the wisdom of the story than let them believe they are secretly at fault.

My story—my ultimate redemption arc—was to *be* the adult who would have likely changed the entire trajectory of my childhood. We do not have to be resigned to our circumstances. As a child of divorce, there is little to no residual emotional damage about whatever went wrong in my parents' relationship. That is not my business, and our kids are also not owed the story and frankly rarely need it. However, they deserve to have parents who recognize that childhood is relatively short, and the fighting in the custody tug-of-war often results in the child losing out. Sometimes parental peace is simply not possible, yet nothing can undo the positive impact of a parent willing to advocate for the rights of their child. To me, the most incredible and valuable plot twist imaginable would be to offer our children an even better childhood than we were given.

#plottwist

13

#getyourownstacy
DOING YOUR INNER WORK

The most profound thing we have to offer our own children is our own healing.
—Anne Lamott

"SERIOUSLY, THOUGH, YOU NEED TO talk to someone," yelled the ten-year-old client to her father. "GET YOUR OWN STACY!"

Narrator: we are 100 percent confident he will not, in fact, get his own therapist. (Can confirm.) My waiting room contained the weighted tension in the air, pointing out that the factual issue at hand had *little* (nothing) to do with her.

Recent generations, exposed to way more social-emotional concepts than '80s and '90s kids, are calling out and therefore not tolerating observed unhealthy patterns. Kids, learning from TikTok, SEL teachings, each other, and the trickle-down impact of others' therapeutic work, have important language (when used accurately) for what they're going through. Somehow, though, the term *gaslighting* has ended up in common teen vernacular, chores are not necessarily "violating a boundary," and every time a person disagrees with you does not equate with manipulation. Just saying.

In 2018, my path led me to a nine-month certification program called SPT, in which my professional career significantly forever shifted. Lisa Dion, an international educator and founder of the Synergetic Play Therapy Training Institute, created Synergetic Play Therapy (SPT), which is now one of the most widely used modalities with children and is used worldwide. SPT, as defined, is a research-informed model of play therapy combining the therapeutic powers of play with nervous system regulation, interpersonal neurobiology, physics, attachment, mindfulness, and therapist authenticity. Becoming certified in the modality fundamentally changed me not only as a clinician but as a person. Of all the trainings ever completed in my two decades as a therapist, there is nothing that has shaped me more than the SPT certification program.

A core principle (and my favorite) of SPT is the therapist's ability to be authentic and congruent. When the clinician has a regulated nervous system, it therefore becomes possible for another to be able to coregulate through the dance of attunement. Basically, we can help one another breathe easier, literally and figuratively.

When a therapist's nonverbal communication and words are congruent, it allows safety and trust to form and helps to be an external regulator for the client. If the therapist is having a hard day but is not good at faking it (because let's face it, kids see through all of that), it doesn't create a sense of safety in the room. It is much more honest to say, "Yes, you might have noticed I am a little tired today, but I am happy to be here with you." It is always important to me to point out that it is not their job to take care of me, and this time is all about giving them the attention and support they need.

A much more in-depth explanation of SPT can be found at SynergeticPlayTherapy.com, but the heartbeat and bottom line of this approach is just to be a genuine person to help kids be authentically themselves. And the process of

Doing Your Inner Work

becoming authentic is to unlearn all that has been taught before that no longer serves us well. Graduate school carried the overt message that to be an effective clinician, one needs to have gotten *all* their life affairs in order. Since that falls far short of realistic, the only other option is to mask and hide one's humanity, which doesn't end well. (I tried.)

Many counseling programs now require students to be in some form of short-term therapy, which to me seems greater than, if not equal to, the benefit of an entire grad school program. All clinicians I know who are engaged in their own life's recovery work are constantly and intentionally becoming the best possible version of themselves. They are, in my opinion, safer humans to work with than those who believe they have arrived. (We all know those people, and they are tough to be around, am I right?)

As Brené Brown states, "If you are not in the arena getting your ass kicked on occasion, I am not interested in or open to your feedback. There are a million cheap seats in the world today filled with people who will never be brave with their own lives but spend every ounce of energy they have hurling advice and judgment at those of us who are trying to dare greatly. If you are criticizing from a place where you're not also putting yourself on the line, I'm not interested in your feedback."[25]

Undoubtedly, the most significant contribution to producing healthier clinicians is putting in emotional elbow grease to become models to emulate. Inner work, being honest with myself, is also for the sake of all the clients in my care. Healing, so that my capacity expands to support the extent of their pain, is worth it for the long haul. The number of times questions come up in sessions about having my own support is countless, and every time, my clients appear relieved that maybe it isn't that bizarre after all to see a therapist. It is yet another reminder there is nothing reprehensible about having a therapist, and that there is nothing inherently wrong with them for having one. When I mention Melissa to my own clients, I tell them she is their grand-therapist—my own made-up term. And they also have a great-grand therapist, as many solid clinicians have their own support in place. It is a rough world out there, guys.

Not too long ago, a young adult client came in distraught, as the previous session had ended with her emotions forming an angry whirlwind that formed some verbal shrapnel. She apologized for the interaction and was very worried her future sessions would be terminated. I told her, "Please. We all have intense feelings, and therapy can be the place for them. Mine were sorted with your grand-therapist on Tuesday." She took a deep breath. (I also added that the only way to really get fired was to intentionally hurt my therapy dog, Willow, so she was in the clear.)

One teenage client worried that I thought they were "crazy" for being in counseling. "Um, I have my own therapist, just so you know," I responded. They looked at me with wide emoji eyes and gasped, "Actually?" Another said, "What do *you* have to talk to a therapist about?" (Oh, my friend, so, so much. We do not have the time nor the snacks available for that dialogue.) My favorite is "Wait, what? A *therapist* needs therapy?"

Yes, all of us, really. It was not an accident that so many of us with significant challenges ended up in the helping professions. Because when you don't have what you need when you are young, many grow to want to offer it to others. My Care Bears who were lined up in a circle for group therapy when I was five didn't heal themselves, people. But Grumpy Bear had a rough road ahead, because, well, people (and stuffies) need to *want* the help.

Normalizing seeking support is happening in witnessing younger generations lift the stigma with each other. It continues to dissipate, as many share how they pass down session insight to their friends, which is the beauty of the current mental health climate. It is in modeling not suffering alone that lives will inevitably be saved, guaranteed. Offering gifted wisdom also contains the trickle-down impact of solid therapeutic support. The gift that keeps on giving includes sharing things that have helped me through the years and telling of strategies that have worked well—and ones that have not.

As Lisa Dion often says regarding play therapy, "The therapist is the most important toy in the room." She has shared at conferences how she watches therapists scatter to buy the best new therapeutic toy or game in the hope that it will best aid in helping a child. While my latest Minecraft magnetic blocks are fabulous, the message here: it is the *therapeutic relationship* that best helps someone heal, not the most updated model of anything.

A healthy therapeutic relationship *can be* the ultimate conduit for healing. Therefore, choose wisely.

As a new college freshman, while my mom was battling breast cancer, I used the resources on the Arizona State campus to seek first-time support. No one my age had any experience, let alone the words, to offer for my situation. At my first appointment, the young clinician asked, "What scares you the most about your mom dying?" I shared that not knowing what the afterlife would look like for her haunted me. The clinician looked at me above her clipboard and asserted, "Well, that is why you are sad. You are making yourself upset thinking like that. Don't do that anymore." Leaving feeling shamed for being honest, my eighteen-year-old self did not attempt therapy until far, far after her death. (*Just don't be sad* is never good advice, for any reason, just in case that is not crystal clear.)

Astonishingly, my student intake session is not a fond memory, nor did it inspire me to try again any time soon. The hardest part of finding the right fit is finding the right fit. With my practice, it is standard to make sure my client, regardless of age, has a say in returning after the initial visit. There do not appear to be benefits to being forced into that scenario. There are a lot of therapists out there, and not everyone clicks with the first one they try. The hope is that in an intake, one can get the best gut-level feel for whether or not it is a relationship worth trying out. Usually in my office it goes well, as I am shorter than most of them and therefore nonthreatening.

Within fifteen minutes of my *own* intake as a client, my current therapist, Melissa, made an impressive body language observation about my demeanor. Blinking and confirming the accuracy, my heart rate went through the roof. Because, what? Since my intention in seeking support was *not* to delve into the past but rather to find strategies to cope with the dysregulation in the present, my thought was that I needed to back away slowly. After the first session, when it was clear there was some deep pain that needed to be attended to, I was the human equivalent of the *Simpsons* meme "Chuckles: I'm in danger." Convinced that my story, my pain, my need was far too much, I attempted to "let her off the hook" in a voice message. Spoiler alert: my strategy was incredibly ineffective. Second, bonus spoiler alert: the panic leading me to reach out had everything to do with the past. So that's been fun.

Here is what I know. Therapy is a confidential place to be truly heard and fully seen. Therapy is a place to practice and develop self-awareness to be a better human. Therapy is an opportunity for validation, to be understood without being interrupted. Therapy, at its best, is ultimately intended to be an incredibly safe space where you can leave breathing easier, loving yourself and others better, and where you can find hope when all is lost.

To feel allowed to tell one's whole messy, unattractive, horrific truth in a safe, nonjudgmental context has no monetary value. Can you imagine, for one who has felt in hiding their literal entire life, how healing that can be for one's self-perception—to be welcomed with open arms? What a difference that would make in the trajectory of one's life?

Being a human is not easy, especially a young one, with little to no power. Sure, kids/teens don't have to pay bills, which can often be the first response when an adult hears of a kid having a hard time. When kids talk about a person in their life who is now getting counseling and is easier to talk to or no longer slamming things while saying they aren't angry at all, it feels like everyone wins. Fewer eggshells and more open honesty? Yes, please.

Also, being able to genuinely apologize to a child when one inevitably makes a valid mistake is the direct result of doing inner work. From my observations over time, I can attest that sincere apologies can absolutely change things, literally overnight. So many times, asking kids, "Did you get an apology for that?" they look at me with shocked irritation. "Um, no." Not having grown up with any apologies in my house, it isn't what was modeled for me either, but rather, witnessing the impact in families where it *has* been makes me believe.

Being accused of stealing something, which a parent perhaps finds later where they last left it, is something that deserves an apology. Yelling at a child, when what we are mad about is really a situation that has nothing to do with the kid, deserves amends. Going back on a promise deserves admitted wrongdoing. We are not talking about lying prostrate on the ground begging for mercy, but rather a sincere acknowledgment of being human, making a mistake, and wanting to do better moving forward. It is communicating just because you are younger doesn't mean that you don't deserve the same dignity when wronged.

The concept of rupture and repair comes from psychoanalytic theory, with the belief that it is in the repair where we find our connection to one another. Many parents come to me feeling remorse about a fight or harsh words shared to their child. In those moments, I remind them that real intimacy in our relationships is found in the ability to rebuild a sense of safety and security. It is not about never hurting one another; it is about recognizing where we went wrong and choosing a restorative path back to a deeper connection.

Sixteen-year-old Nathan's dad reached out because his son refused to engage with him, period. He shared they had been close before the divorce, but after, Nathan became estranged and no longer wanted to spend any time at his home. Knowing that Nathan's pain originated from specific words exchanged in the process of his parents' divorce, my questions to the father were about whether his conversations ever ended in trying to make amends. He asked me if it would help, and we talked about how there was little downside to genuinely trying. After they made a time to meet in a park, one meeting was a bridge on the way back to each other, formed by bricks of genuine remorse.

Scenarios that result from supportive therapy include but are not limited to the following:

- Young children whose anger regularly reaches disproportionate levels and start to learn Dan Siegal's "name it to tame it" approach to regulate their bodies.
- Tweens who know how to recognize beginning depressive symptoms and therefore engage in healthy coping strategies instead of dangerously hiding them.
- Teens who seek help for self-harming behaviors because they no longer want others to know automatically of their struggles when they wear a swimsuit.
- Young adults who are able to identify toxic relationship sequences and find ways to interrupt the pattern before years of pain accumulate.
- Parents who no longer want to repeat the stories inflicted upon them as children that continue to linger. They want to find better ways to communicate, connect, and cherish their own kids.
- Grandparents who want to understand why family members have gone "no-contact" with them and want to begin to do better, as it is not yet too late.

So many of my friends have joked that they could have used a Stacy when they were ten. And I always respond with, "Yeah, well *Stacy* needed a Stacy."

If my story had been different at age five, a sharp therapist would have been able to identify sexual abuse taking place, in likely record time.

If my story had been different at age ten, a skilled therapist would have helped me heal from the abuse and offered guidance to my mom, who had none available to her.

If my story had been different at age thirteen, a compassionate therapist would have been a safe place to escape to, following the horrors experienced in Utah.

If my story had been different at age sixteen, a wise therapist would have helped me navigate the anticipatory grief of watching my mom slowly die.

If my story had been different at age twenty-two, a solid therapist would have helped me sift through feelings regarding the death of my mom.

We are doing our kids a disservice when we *just* call them resilient but do not offer the support they deserve. This is not limited to counseling; it can be in the form of support in being able to show up and listen without our own inner noise taking over the scene.

Stacy's young soul was incredibly resilient, *and also,* her journey would not have been remotely as painful with the right care, guaranteed. In my beloved Refuge community, where I serve as the kids and families cultivator, our motto is "No one does hard stuff alone." My wish would be for everyone who wants mental health support to be able to access the right resources. There is no question that there is not equity in health care, which is in part the idea of this book. You don't have to be in therapy to do your own healing work, but there is so much to be said about having a safe, trained professional on your team. Many will never be able to bring a child in to see a clinician, however, so for all to have access to a little guidance and some extra insight *is* equal opportunity.

As for me? My clients, rest assured that Melissa, your grand-therapist, is relentless in her commitment to help the most wounded parts of me heal. Encouraging me to say incredibly hard things that get stuck in my throat, seeing me when I want to hide, and having important conversations to heal old wounds, all happen regularly. Therefore, you are getting an actively healing clinician who practices what she preaches, identifies her blind spots, *and also* has her own ass in the ring to be challenged, supported, and emotionally held. We all deserve that level of support, really.

#getyourownstacy #oramelissa #orasomeone

14

#hellodarknessmyoldfriend
DEPRESSION IS A REPEAT OFFENDER

Sometimes living means burning the fire escapes.
—Andrea Gibson

ICE SKATING FOR THE FIRST time in college resulted in completely shattering my right ankle, taking medical leave for a semester, and two subsequent, long surgeries. Translation, in case you missed it: I am *clearly* incredible at said sport. On a Saturday in my sophomore year of college, my friends lured me away from studying for a science test to go ice skating. "Because Arizona is so hot, because you study too much, because you have never been! It will be fun," they said. Which literally could not have been more ominous, and let this be a lesson to stay in school, kids. My dorm manager, as I whizzed out the lobby doors said—no joke—"Have fun! Don't break your ankle!"

Returning home wheelchair-bound was not the satisfying conclusion to our evening. Because I clearly cannot do anything halfway, my ankle break was incredibly complex and somehow fascinating to the hospital staff. Cool. My skate got caught in a groove in the ice, one of my guy friends came up behind me, grabbed my waist to be funny (hilarious), and the snap was loud enough to alert even the fancy professional in the middle of the arena. After being rushed by ambulance to the hospital, the x-ray showed that my tibia and fibula broke *each other* in the fall. Surgery resulted in seven screws, a plate, and nail installation. Several years later, my bones were still growing over the metal, so they had to scrape my bones and remove the hardware. Again, I was committed to the bit. However, because of this remaining ankle instability and despite being five feet four, I remain ineligible to wear high heels. The horrors never cease. At least my clients enjoy knowing when they hit about seventh grade, they will typically tower over me, so there's that. When the weather is cold here in Colorado, my ankle aches, and when one of my clients talks about ice skating, I make sure not to welcome Debbie Downer to the chat.

However, my ankles are, as you know, always with me, and therefore forever relevant. One of my closest friends, Erika, and I recently went to a summertime Stevie Nicks concert. #amazing. However, my right ankle started wildly throbbing inside my cleverly disguised orthotic shoe by the time we found our seats in the giant event center. Leaning over to her as we finished the climb, I grumbled that it was so irritating that despite the injury and subsequent surgeries being two decades prior, the throbbing was still a recurring issue. She, my beloved, deep Enneagram 4 friend, mused, "Isn't that so validating, though, in terms of emotional pain? Like even if the hurt was so long ago, it still aches?" Yes, yes it is, Erika.

Just the other day, my thoughts quickly spiraled down what felt like a mental rabbit hole. Not unlike Alice's beginning journey in Wonderland, it felt disorienting and poorly lit. No quirky tea party or eerily smiling Cheshire Cat; instead, all-consuming depressive thoughts and uncomfortable feelings. However, my spirit was anything but alarmed—in fact, quite the contrary. Profound darkness felt natural, and my body easily acclimated to the mood temperature drop. Despair is familiar. Trustworthy, even.

Writing from the eye of the storm, showing up without yet having all the answers—albeit feeling discouraged—presents an opportunity to write when the dark is very fresh and inky thick. When I was a young adult, reading about depression in self-help books, it seemed as if the authors usually had only experienced occasional bad days. Never did I feel fully understood from the actual depths of despair. Never did I hear from an author who navigated fiery waves of hopelessness without drowning, who didn't heal their burns overnight, and yet was able to still be a functional member of society.

I'm reminded of the Rumi quote that says, "When setting out on a journey, do not seek advice from those who have never left home." While there is always room to hold space without personal experience, the feeling of being understood without words is unparalleled. Please note that #hellodarknessmyoldfriend is intentionally meant to come later in this book, past the earlier chapter called #denyingthedragon: demystifying suicidal ideation. Highlighting the reality that depression often returns is crucial in supporting someone who suffers with both anxiety and despondency. And it is in the recurrence that many become *more* lost and feel concerned that they used up all their punches on their emotional support cards.

Talking to my dear friend Sherrey about my next session with my own therapist, Melissa, was evidence of this double standard. I mentioned it would be the first time to verbalize a particularly hard story with Melissa, and it was a necessary hard memory to detox from. Doubting myself in my unnecessary attempts to not be overly dramatic, I said, "I mean, I have said that it is a *hard* one before." She replied, "The frequency doesn't change the validity."

The frequency doesn't change the validity.

The message: there's no quota when we are talking matters of life or death. We must not, covertly or overtly, communicate that staying in a dark place holds a greater value than the pride of asking for help.

Teens navigate the confusion of adolescence by identifying with TikTok trends and Instagram reels, and my office walls have contained so many conversations about the latest trends/drama/omg you will never believe what happened/here for my spilling the tea session. Not to hate on social media, as there are for sure distinct benefits to living with so much accessibility. Some of my very best decisions have come directly from being connected via internet/social media—my move to Colorado, connecting to communities that enhance my life, and finding my beloved therapist, to name just a few—so there is no shade thrown, at all. However, there are absolutely downfalls to having so much accessibility. It is an incredibly mixed bag, as the internet is wide and bottomless. On your teen's For You page (the algorithm's best guess about the viewer's desired content), there could be videos of baby owls mixed with mental health tips, everything from funny reels to teens engaging in harmful behaviors. Many teens report they watch videos in between therapy sessions to get a little extra support. While some older generations would be baffled by this statement, the reality is that our kids are connected to each other in ways that previous generations did not have the opportunity to be. A double-edged sword, for sure. But when a kid shows me how they built my office in Minecraft to increase their comfort level in therapy, it makes me see that the kids are all right. In addition, they had amazing design choices, especially the amethyst they mined. Exactly what the creators of Minecraft envisioned, in fact.

In private practice since 2009, I have had multiple clients on my caseload see me throughout different chapters of life.

While it ages me, being able to hold space for a young adult who first saw me while they were in middle school is truly an honor. To be a safe place to land through various life challenges means that kids returning home from college for the holidays get to be seen and known all over again. It means that when the stress intensifies senior year, one knows where to turn. It means that when a season comes where a therapist is less needed, I am able to say, "You know where to find me. Not going anywhere; my walls are solidly purple." And believe it or not, they really are.

Also, some clients, with teary eyes when it comes time to tapering off frequent counseling, explain their emotional dilemmas related to leaving. On numerous occasions, clients have said they are scared that if they leave, then ask to come back later, a parent may question them and insinuate they've failed somehow at mental health. Also: that is not a thing. If you are alive, you have the opportunity to fight the good fight with the rest of us.

If there is one ask of parents, it is that kids will not be met with extreme alarm if they ask to go back to their therapist.

The desire needs to be celebrated, and a solid clinician will let you know if there is reason to be extremely concerned. To me, this request is ironically less one to be alarmed by than the kid who you cannot even tell at face value is struggling. *That* to me is the scariest—the kids who have it "together" and never ask for a thing. Having been one of those kids, I know that it remains impossible for others to help you find a way out again if they do not know you are lost.

Avery, sixteen, was a client of mine since she was in middle school, throughout different chapters in her story. There are significant challenges she has faced, including suicidality, (really) mean girl drama, and being in the middle of her parents' incredibly high-conflict divorce. The fight over parenting time appears never-ending, and it is exhausting even thinking about the effort both of them have put into fighting this battle.

Having open communication with both parents has been crucial in supporting Avery, and they are on the same page related to her frequency with counseling. However, one of the parents said to me one day, "Why is she not all better? Why has she seen you so long and still has depression and sometimes the desire to die?" Pointing out the significant obstacles in Avery's way, including her parents often needing police to facilitate conflict at either house or with each other, helped shed light on the issues. I said, "Well, Avery is continually faced with challenging circumstances, and there has not been any time to not live in crisis mode. She needs stability, and when that happens, her chances of being able to manage continue to increase." Avery has been doing the best she can, with circumstances swirling around her, but has not had moments where things were predictable in either household. One cannot fully heal in an environment in which one is still getting hurt. It just doesn't work that way. For Avery, the dark is a reliable constant. The darkness is always, well, dark. And while feeling terrible is less than ideal, it offers more appeal than poking one's head out to hear the yelling and the chaos.

Life, though, also shows us that it is unpredictable, full of both wonder and sorrow, and never stops with challenges. Like, ever. As Pema Chödrön writes in *When Things Fall Apart*, "To be fully alive, fully human, and completely awake is to be continually thrown out of the nest."[26] Depression as a diagnosis is treatable, but there is no guarantee that future events and circumstances will not activate what may have been dormant inside one's psyche. If anything is heard in this chapter, it is this: just because depression reemerges does not negate all the effort one has put forth to fight the darkness.

Your child, your friend, your person whom you deeply care about may really not know how to ask for help and be afraid to scare you with the depth of felt sadness.

I know this from not only so many depressed clients but my own personal experience battling depression. We know not everyone who is sad, lonely, or somehow otherwise suffering is receiving the messages they need from the people who could best offer them. Not every person has found the safe community they deserve, especially our kids. When out in the real world and a spotted mental health message is on an article of clothing or item, my internal cheer squad goes wild. In fact, owning several hoodies with suicide prevention messages feels like my own intentional act of resistance against despair. My latest lilac hoodie says on the back, "Stay here, the world needs you in it." If one person on the brink of despair happens to read it when we cross paths and is able to hold on because they feel they are too much, not enough, or a combination, then my money has been well spent. And since most of the time we will never know how our attempts to help strangers turn out, my vote is to consider it as always contributing to the greater good in the world. As one who may always be in depression recovery, it is not news that even professionals have challenges articulating feelings in self-reflection.

Despite there being countless campaigns to remove the stigma of mental health, the issue, in my observation, can begin at home, in social circles, and with one's close friends. It starts with realizing that general campaigns for any cause take action for the greater good but can miss the mark right in front of us. The proverb "The cobbler's kids have no shoes" is based around the idea that someone with a particular skill set (communication, for instance) can become too busy to have hard conversations with the people in their own life. For the life of me, I will never understand how when I was a child, one of my mom's dental patients would call our home to speak to her about an eating disorder. My mom spent hours on the phone with this teenage girl, and as I quietly played with puzzles in my room, I wondered how this person chose my mom to be a listening ear. Believe me when I tell you that there is not a single instance I can recall my mom guiding me in literally anything to do with feelings, issues, or life challenges. Not one.

Much of my own pain froze in time when it was impossible to feel what was needed. The intention of my entire career is to help younger generations not carry a lifetime of suffering with them like an ever-increasing weight. To be able to deal with issues in real time, without building an identity around the worst part of their story. I wonder who I would be if any of my circumstances had been even remotely different. To be honest, that thought pattern makes me incredibly, incredibly sad, so I do not stay there for long.

My incredible therapist, Melissa, points out how the severe psychological abuse I endured as a child formed my sense of self, making it a confusing mess of what to believe. If younger me, bravely squeaking the words, had been heard, there is no question that the dark would not be as appealing now. Had one safe adult, holding a flashlight and my hand, led me to see that there was much more to life than the trauma, my story would be a different one. This is why our kids need more than just therapists to walk alongside them. They deserve a community made up of all kinds of people to build a foundation of safety. My mom kept me moderately isolated, so there were no other social safety nets to catch what was happening at home. In school, they didn't worry about the kids identified as "gifted." I was identified in kindergarten as "academically talented," and yet I can't help but wonder if my scholastic abilities masked my emotional needs in a way that kept me far under the radar of concern.

Neurodivergence for the win, but more importantly, we have a greater awareness now that grades are only one piece of the puzzle. In the past decade or so, there has been a growing awareness of how autism shows up in girls. Since girls historically often mask their behavior more easily than boys, autism in females was missed more in previous decades than it is today. So many more kids are getting the support they need because of our societal awareness, and I find that incredibly encouraging. We are trying to pave a better way for our kids to move forward in a world more emotionally intelligent, more connected, and much more secure.

There was not one time in my childhood in which emotional security was a theme, and instead, the reel in my head now is how to create more of that for the kids in my orbit.

Do I wish that my memories of horrific experiences could be deleted and replaced with a safe, protected, and loving childhood? Obviously. Since life doesn't offer that feature for any of us, it is simply not an option. However, a speculative fiction book called *Tell Me an Ending* that I read several years ago made me rethink that fantasy quite a lot. It is not an exaggeration to tell you this book's story line swims around my brain at least once a week. Set in an imagined future, the premise is that thousands of people suddenly get a notice they can get a memory back that they once paid to remove.[27] Insert wide-eyed emoji.

All the characters' story endings leave you doubtful that the whole process of removal was a wise one in the first place. Who would we be without the memories, even the brutal ones? Is the dark actually a way in which we can befriend sadness, instead of trying to destroy it? If given the opportunity to delete a year of my life (go big or go home), would

Depression Is a Repeat Offender

I take it? What if that meant gaps would be confusing yet the pain of remembering no longer haunted me? Is the dark so familiar that we would choose it over the wild unknown? When it comes to our kids, my experience is that, yes, they know the dark, and the light holds too much hope that can get shattered. One teen told me that it was disappointing when they came out of a depressive episode to find that the same circumstances, both internal and external, still existed.

In the suicide prevention guide entitled *How I Stayed Alive When My Brain Was Trying to Kill Me*, the author writes, "Although my life was filled with chaos, it was familiar chaos, which gave me the feeling that I had some control over it. This was an illusion."[28] In my observation, kids/teens have looked at what life is offering them, which is not guaranteed, and have gone right back into their pillow forts. But the black, you see, is always, always black. To Write Love on Her Arms, a powerful nonprofit dedicated to helping people find resources for dealing with depression and suicidality, has created meaningful slogans to spread their message. This year holds a new favorite: "Heal out loud. We almost lost you in silence."

Glennon Doyle has always written openly and honestly about her battles with anxiety and depression and has helped normalize these battles. In her bestseller *Untamed*, she describes a strategy to combat dark moments.[29] In 2015, she blogged (remember that?) about her concept called "The Erasing." Her technique is to write letters from her Up Self to her Down Self, and vice versa. A practice Glennon created encourages people to write messages from their "higher self" (Up Self) to their more vulnerable, insecure self (Down Self) to help navigate complicated emotions. This concept is so beautiful to me, because we can forget in the hard moments all the good there is in our worlds. And conversely, it is helpful to journal while in the mental space of the Down Self (especially for the therapists) so that we don't dismiss our feelings as simply having a bad day. We can easily forget how dark things got once the light is turned back on. And yet, dealing with the core of what was happening when things feel extra challenging can make depressive episode remission less mysterious.

My teenage clients are encouraged to document their feelings close to the time they are experiencing them and bring those notes to therapy. I cannot adequately express how proud it makes me not only when they remember to jot things down but when they bring that rich data to their session. Whipping out their notes on their phones or hardcover journals, they have captured in real time the breadth and depth of their emotional experience. It is much more productive to identify the emotions and release them, as opposed to reporting, "IDK. It was, like, a bad day or whatever." Give me something to work with, people.

What we *can* teach kids is that they have a bottomless internal reservoir of strength within, which no one can remotely touch. While trapped in Utah, there was nothing solid for me to cling to. No ability to ask for help, nobody who would stop the abuse, no one to listen, no one to ensure that basic human rights were not being violated. What made me smirk to myself, however, was knowing they could not control one.single.thing that happened in my head. My mind was literally untouchable, and due to that, survival became possible. Had there been an inability to escape mentally, my sanity irrefutably would not have had a chance.

Victor Frankl eloquently also talks about this power in his autobiographical *Man's Search for Meaning*. Frankl was a prisoner in a Nazi concentration camp and lived to write about choosing a way to imagine a better future, despite unspeakable circumstances. "We who lived in concentration camps can remember the men who walked through the huts comforting others, giving away their last piece of bread. They may have been few in number, but they offer sufficient proof everything can be taken from a man but one thing: the last of the human freedoms—to choose one's attitude in any given set of circumstances, to choose one's own way."[30]

Now, in a similar vein to #andalso, it is important not to invalidate the magnitude of traumatic, horrific, unimaginable experiences. It also means showing that there is more to their identity and sense of self than just being depressed. My therapist often uses the Internal Family Systems approach, which is the theory that our identity is made up of different parts. When telling her once how depressed I felt, she had me get curious about whether that was all of me or just a part. Because when it is not the *entirety* of your being experiencing that absence of light, it becomes much more bearable.

Finding our way despite the dark isn't denial; it is choosing another way out. It is showing up for our kids/friends/people when it is bleak and pointing to the hope of a better tomorrow. It is not making reality appear to be shinier than it really is, because let's face it: some things are just hard and scary and can feel impossible. However, if there is even one adult showing up for a child, there is counsel to navigate the unlit territory. If we can offer opportunities for real connection, solid support, and faithful guidance, the dark will begin to lose some of its charm. Noah Kahan sings along these lines, reminding us the darkness can be misleading, and the lights can always be turned back on.

#hellodarknessmyoldfriend

15

#teeth
FAMILY VALUES

I hope you believe that you can still make a beautiful life for yourself even if you lost many years of it to grief, or darkness, or a wound that wouldn't close.
—Yung Pueblo

IF YOU ASKED ME AS a child what my family valued most, the confident answer would have been "teeth." As a passionate dental hygienist, my mom was very clear: no greater sin existed than not flossing before bed. A library fine was a close second. Only while checking for cavities/gum decay/braces alignment did my mom ever actually touch me. While that feels unbearably sad to write, it felt normal at the time, with no comparison offered. Constantly brushing, flossing, and doing all else in my power to earn my mom's affection, still nothing ever hit the mark. But you better believe I tried.

Memo received loud and clear: dental health meant literally *everything*. My dear friend Erika pointed out once it was an actual dark comedy—so many horribly tragic things were happening in my family, yet all the focus was on . . . teeth? To me, it makes one curious: Is it worth it to have a child who is internally suffering but scores brownie points with the orthodontist? Who wins if the teen has zero cavities yet does not feel safe in her body? One who faithfully flosses but is silently slipping through the cracks with depression? My mom *constantly* stressed the importance of a first impression smile, yet she failed to notice how disingenuous the one was on her only child's face.

It also raises the question, What *truly* matters, at the end of the day? Because if given the choice of security, support, safety, or even . . . infrequent hugs instead, younger me would have laid out a welcome mat for a cavity party. Sure, my smile was sparkly, but when your insides don't match your outsides, it comes at a cost. Unironically, Melissa Manchester's melody "Don't Cry Out Loud" plays softly in the background reel of my childhood memories. The song spoke to me early on, and by kindergarten, my artificial grin was practically perfected.

While multitudes of variables exist, exercises in missing the point can surface in families, to obviously differing degrees. *Everyone* wants to present a favorable image to the world, because of course we do. Our survival has always been dependent on following social mores, so nothing new. Charles Darwin's 1869 research is often misquoted as stating that "only the strongest survive." But what he uncovered was that the species that survives is the one most *adaptable* to its environment, which is much more nuanced. We come by it honestly, and people often are doing the best they can, at any given moment. But it is when we are desperately dying inside that the bigger problem exists. When there are gaping familial wounds and the people inside are trapped in shame, it creates a damaging disconnect.

There was an incredibly lovely family that came to me years ago with a complicated situation involving their two children. Fortunate enough to work individually with their ten-year-old daughter, we unpacked the issue together, with intentional delicacy. Learning, however, that the family had completely hunkered down and told no one else about the situation concerned me. The mom had explained to me they were afraid of losing not only their best friends, their extended family support, but everyone else in their circles. They subsequently canceled vacation plans with friends, withdrew from small groups, and even considered moving towns. Now the situation was tangled, but in my opinion, it was a disproportionate response that further served to alienate them. Close friends were not even given the *opportunity* to show up for them in ways that could have been meaningful and healing. The belief was that no one would support them, and they acted on that thought as if it was fact. While there admittedly could have been responses that were less than favorable, the desire to look like the perfect family only served to isolate and eventually add to the family's secret shame.

Also, it is important to note: everyone in our lives is not entitled to everything. Of course, we have many relationships that will not be given access to our trickiest challenges. There are deeply painful memories shared with my therapist that will never be communicated to anyone else. Ever. What is critical, however, is that we have deeply honest relationships that are fully aware of what we are moving through. My closest people know the general outline of what is being stirred up for me in therapy, but the details are left for Melissa alone. She is lucky that way.

In some casual discussions over time with friends about both overt and covert messages they received as children regarding family values, the variety of feedback became quite interesting. The inventory included, but was not limited to, athletic ability, the need to be seen as "good," grades, religion, kindness at any cost, even to yourself, busyness, sacrifice, being presentable at all times, appearing to be financially well-off, professional accolades, lawns (to which another friend responded, "Your dad *does* care an awful lot about lawns"), comedic talent, and the bottom line: image.

Again, none of these are inherently wrong, and conversely, each has a level of importance in a functional society. It is, however, devastating when a teen literally struggling with an addiction to self-harm gets scolded for a B on a physics test. Or when a child is getting severely bullied at school but is told at home to tell no one, because "we aren't a family of complainers." Or a family who is showing up at church on Sunday saying they are "blessed" but truly believes they are somehow *cursed.*

Rhiannon, twelve, came to therapy riddled with debilitating anxiety impacting every aspect of her life. Her mom, who happened to be the coach of the sports team Rhiannon played for, expressed concern about her daughter's lack of performance at the most recent tournament. Part of the conversation involved psychoeducation for the family about anxiety's impact on the brain. The rest of our chat included a gentle lead toward seeing Rhiannon was really suffering and the sport might have to take a backseat for her mental health to improve.

Family therapy: it's as fun as it sounds. In all seriousness, though, if given a safe enough container, magical things can happen when people start to listen to each other. Amazing things emerge when people know they will not be interrupted. The sentiment "I never knew you felt that way. Thank you for saying that" never gets old to me. Necessary, however, is a talking ball, which in my office is a tiny Squishmallow. The key to supervising these heated discussions is to prohibit my stuffed pink bird from being chucked directly at someone's head. In my sessions, we absolutely end on a positive note, and each participant is asked to respond to an uplifting prompt.

Always at the edge of my awareness is the reality that had *my* family sought therapy when I was a teen, there would have been zero chance of my honest participation. My mom was too emotionally fragile, and it was already a delicate situation with most conversations. Knowing in family therapy that one goes home with the people with whom they enter the room, my comments would have undoubtedly been surface-level responses. Being cognizant a similar dynamic exists in many families, I consider my questions and potential depth of approach carefully. Family secrets come to light often in family therapy, as obviously part of the foundation of the problems. My family, like many, knew a thing or two about secrets, on multiple levels.

Finding out a decade ago, per 23andMe, that I'm 99.6 percent Ashkenazi Jew came as a bit of a surprise revelation. After my mom died, it was revealed she secretly held that knowledge close and harbored a deep-seated fear about what that could mean in a racist world. The secrecy meant food was hidden in my house that was considered Jewish, a gold cross was worn my entire childhood, despite being raised in an agnostic home, and I was told through gritted teeth to "make.it.up" when twice faced with a family tree assignment.

(In the unlikely chance any of my elementary school-teachers read this, apologies for the fraudulent documents.)

Therefore, the resistance movement of WW2 was the only part of history that thoroughly fascinates me. #obsessed. My lovely book club friends generously indulge my historical fiction selections and continually encourage me to choose reading that lights me up. Give me a story about a badass female spy conspiring to defeat Nazis, and the five-star review has already written itself.

My amazing friend Dawn, born the same year as my mom, has consistently been a source of wisdom to me for seventeen years. She explained once that since their childhood was so close to the Holocaust years, it made sense my mom was paranoid about anti-Semitism. And yet one wonders if the emphasis on secrecy created an unnecessary foundation for shame, and if there could have been a better way?

The awareness of my cultural makeup is deeply uncomfortable to internalize (and honestly write about). There is no doubt the discomfort in even talking about it is due to years of being afraid of being accused of something that would put both of us in perceived danger. My mom lived as if everyone we knew could turn on us, not unlike what happened across Europe in the 1940s. Yet this level of alarm used up her ability to feel safe with anyone, so she chose not to have friends, out of fear it could end in betrayal. Imagine how confusing that was for me as a kid—to be told that even though you weren't Jewish, anyone at any time could report you for anything, and you would be killed. At the time it made sense, but as one ages, we see things a lot more clearly with different, older eyes. And now I feel deeply sad for my mom, who lived her entire life feeling at the precipice of danger.

Generational trauma, also known as ancestral trauma, refers to the passing down of traumatic experiences or stressors from one generation to another. Some of this can literally be through DNA, and some from stories or witnessed trauma. The only factual piece given in my childhood was that my grandmother emigrated as a child from Wales. When we have more data, the next generation can breathe easier and help inform the present. Identifying patterns and behaviors and therefore learning better ways to approach situations help everyone to feel safer. When parents tell me they want to do things differently than their own parents—*not* yelling as much, *not* modeling drinking to cope, *not* slamming doors when angry—these are statements to be celebrated. In addition, they say they want to add different approaches than they saw growing up: to praise their kids more, to acknowledge and apologize when a mistake is made, and to try to listen without reacting. These are also remarkable ways to create new familial patterns.

———

Nineteen-year-old Hannah realized she was gay early in high school. As a young adult coming from a Christian home, she was deeply afraid to communicate with her dad, due to his strong religious convictions. She decided, back then, to be brave and share with him her feelings and thoughts on sexuality. He predictably exploded, and their relationship is now extremely strained, at best. Now, one's moral beliefs are their own and extremely personal. No one gets to decide for another how and what to believe. However, when one claims to love another unconditionally, the very *definition* negates conditions.

Perhaps controversial opinion: if religion requires you to disown/abandon/alienate your child, it appears it is time to reevaluate the approach. It would be argued that it is not hate, rather a devotion to a higher power. Yet if people you claim to love are less connected to you due to their beliefs about their own sexuality, everyone loses. You can only pick one: devotion to beliefs or an acceptance. It makes sense to some to say they are holding fast to accept their values, but then it simply cannot be a mystery when a child goes no-contact when they are old enough to do so. It can't be both ways.

Psychiatrist Gabor Maté states, "We're born with a need for attachment and a need for authenticity." We need and deserve both and look for relationships that offer both. If a person feels invalidated for whatever reason, they will not gravitate toward a relationship that perpetuates that system.

From a faith perspective, it makes sense when one believes a certain way, *and yet*, if the value of those principles supersedes the desire to understand a teen on the LGBTQ+ spectrum, the natural consequences are written in the sand.

Sixteen-year-old Liam, reported to the high school counselor for self-harm and subsequent suicidal statements, was referred to me for a higher level of care. When his mom reluctantly brought him to my office, she emphasized they were a Christian family and his "sinful behavior" toward his body did not reflect their values. In the beginning of his fifth session, she stormed into my office, already yelling. She shrieked, "You need to do *something* about this f****t, and *that* is what is wrong with him!" I gently told her we do not use that language here and guided her to my waiting room, with a promise to have a productive conversation with her son.

After reminding him it was a confidential place to express himself, Liam loudly sobbed. His mom found out he was attracted to another boy via taking his phone and proceeded to call him every vile name possible. While he was in the safety of my office, we could talk through strategies to manage his urges to cut again (shocking) and how to ground himself when the panic reemerges. And yet? One cannot manifest a different environment they return to, and that is why some may simply not feel better until they are out of the home.

Luckily for him, conversion therapy, in which a practitioner attempts to change someone's mind about their sexual identity or gender, is now illegal. Not that it would be an option in my office, as my personal belief is nothing is inherently wrong with him. But the ways he is managing to cope could use some adjusting. He expressed he just wished his mom could love him despite his homosexuality, and the ache he expressed was palpable. My heart echoes that wish, and it is such a missed opportunity not to see beyond what she disapproves of. And honestly? The sexuality piece is just one facet, and by rejecting one part of her son, she will miss the entire package.

His mom handed me a check, which included a message about Jesus in the upper left-hand corner. Confidently knowing the messages in the Bible are not hateful and mean-spirited leads me to believe there might be a rupture in interpretation. Observation: if one is trying to instill beliefs in children, they must be congruent messages. You cannot expect a young person, raised on words like "Love each other just as much as I have loved you" and "Love is patient, love is kind" to understand the discrepancy when they are being screamed at that they have become unlovable. This is not to say that one must agree with choices, but it is imperative one tries to understand, if the end result desired is connection. If the hope is to have a close connection with a person, the actions simply do not hold the same weight. But if we are to be in a meaningful relationship with anyone, denying them dignity is not the path to attachment.

The nonprofit Free Mom Hugs exists for this reason and has a goal of "changing the world by simply showing up." They do not seek to replace family relationships, rather to display love and celebration for the LGBTQ+ community as a model of how to do so. They are there to provide affection and encouragement to those who now have no relatives to lean on for support, due to their family's value system. Due to perceived unresolvable differences, some young adults no longer have a place to go for the holidays, contact on birthdays or celebratory events, or any family member as an emergency contact. As one who had no actual living family since being a young adult, the idea of severing a relationship with a living person due to sexuality grieves the deepest part of me.

Family Values

There are pictures of the Free Mom Hugs team embracing a tearful young person, who is likely not experiencing the level of support they deserve in their family. Their efforts to fill some gaps for youth are beautiful—also serving as a reminder that there is still time, while people are alive, to do the repairs necessary to restore relationships. One of their missions is to provide resources to family members and allies so they can be reconciled. My wish for families in these situations is to find their way to each other again, as uncomfortable as it may be. If that is through family counseling, further education and exploration, or even a mediated conversation—there can be a way through. While people are still alive, there is hope.

Katie, my dear friend and amazing travel partner, is an example to me about how to model this level of unconditional love. Her youngest child was diagnosed with a variety of mental illnesses years ago. In addition, they realized in the tween years that they did not fit the mold for society's interpretation of female. Now fifteen, her kid uses they/them pronouns, actively participates in their own therapy, and rejects all attempts at being put in a box. Katie continues to learn all she can about mental illness, sexuality, gender, and what she can do as a parent to remain close to her child. Has this been confusing and sometimes completely frustrating for Katie to understand, as one without these challenges? Obviously. However, Katie's highest values remain connection, understanding, and devotion to her people, and she chooses to educate herself instead of alienating her teen in any way.

Being consulted about tips for family unification, one of my go-to strategies is the idea of a family motto. Having a conversation as a family about focusing on what is important can be centering and offers some hope. After assigning one family the task of agreeing on a motto, they proudly returned the following week with photos. They had decided on "We are strong, and we make good choices." They also strategized to demonstrate this by keeping a jar in the family room with nails. Any time they came home with a story about making a good, strong choice, a nail was added to the jar. Brilliant. For Kathy, my honorary mom, and her family, the saying "Ohana—No one left behind" is used. It also can take away the emphasis on the hard, to what is going well. Big fan.

One of the covert mottos in my family of origin was "Never *ever* ask for help." (Is that why it remains difficult to seek support? It remains a mystery.) My maternal grandmother, who died when I was ten, sternly told me, "There is no such thing as a free lunch. Never owe anyone *anything*. Everyone wants something from you in return." (But The Refuge, my beloved healing community, offers free lunch to the unhoused community three days a week, so . . . ?) It was instilled within me to trust no one (but, um, childhood itself handed me that lesson, thanks) and to keep my thoughts and feelings to myself. It is almost as if my career path wrote itself.

Framed in my office are the wise words of Aibileen Clark in *The Help*: "You is smart. You is kind. You is important." The movie—powerful on multiple levels—showed connection between a small child and her nanny as a healing conduit when her mom berated her at every turn. Mottos can be reinvented, and while we may not have received what we needed at the time, there are opportunities to continue to heal along the way. We can't redo our childhoods (pros and cons to that), but we can find ways to create new regular habits and deeply beneficial thoughts.

For my birthday this year, my dear friend Sherrey got me this "Empowering and Sassy" deck of affirmation cards, and they are my favorite. Now always used to start my day, my current favorite on display is "It's okay to ask for help. You don't have to do it all on your own." (Seeeeee, Grandma?) It is never too late to create new mantras and mottos, and in my opinion, it is one of the healthiest things to do to recreate value within. My current work is to jackhammer false beliefs that contributed to a maladaptive mental foundation and intentionally practice mantras to align with my values. I help kids in a similar process, with relief in knowing their negative beliefs haven't had the time to sink too deep just yet. That helps.

Confession: the other day, my teeth were used to open a package, my therapist was told about my Jewish heritage, and it was manifested—my desired (created) family motto of "There is enough room for me here." And if you are reading this, it means that the world did not in fact spontaneously and dramatically end.

#teeth

16

#fromtheotherside
WHAT KIDS WISH GROWN-UPS KNEW

"You may have critics," said the horse.
"You don't have to be one of them."
—Charles Mackesy

WITH LOVE FROM A CHILDREN'S Therapist: #lessonsIhavelearnedalongtheway was first conceived after listening to similar themes emerge week after week, session after session. Conversations with kids about their perceived challenges don't regularly fall under mandated reporting requirements. (To those not familiar, the limits requiring reporting to authorities include if someone says they are going to hurt themselves, they are going to hurt someone else, or someone is hurting them.) Also, most of what is said does not register as urgent or crucial to share.

In the first session with kids/teens, as well as the parental intake, my policy is that I do not directly quote kids in session updates, but I will share the general subject we talked about, or something I said. To honor the sacred sharing in sessions, this is crucial, as kids would be reluctant to share if their words were just repeated verbatim. They simply wouldn't talk, as they would feel like their privacy was being violated. But, translating what we talked about happens, and I often wish that others could hear directly from kids in the ways I do. Always encouraged is for kids/teens to share with their grown-up what they shared or learned, as there are powerful thoughts that don't need to just stay with me. From the other side of the couch, there has been so much untapped wisdom, excellent points silenced by the ethics of confidentiality.

After unofficially collecting thoughts through the years, I began officially asking the following three questions for this chapter: "What do you wish the adults in your life would stop doing? What do you which they would *start* doing? What do want them to *continue* to do?" Here are some of those responses.

They want to be *seen*.
"I wish my mom saw how hard I try to do the right things."

Often, kids will tell me they are never seen doing something "good," and it seems like the "bad" things are the only ones ever observed. Things going well just seem like givens, but kids tell me that it would be nice to hear more affirmations anyway. Praising kids in front of their parents is my hobby, because who does not want to make two people happy at the same time? (I am who I am.) Really, though, I believe in affirming kids at every opportunity. Just don't make it weird.

One of our primal needs: to be seen for our true intentions. We also have fundamental longings, among others, to be understood, to belong, and to be accepted. Kids can be so prone to peer pressure, as forced membership in a tween social club feels superior to feeling out of place anywhere else. Influencers on social media tend to send the message, "I see you, I get you, buy this product to be like us," and it *works*. No one wants to move through the world invisible (well, for long periods, that is), and kids especially crave group belonging. The more we say, "I see who you are at your core," the less likely they are to define themselves through someone else's lens.

They want to be *heard*.
"I wish I could talk to my dad without feeling like he is going to blow up at any second."

Teens tell me all the time that they desire to share things they think or feel, but it is the potential for an unpleasant reaction that stops them in their tracks. A recent trend (hope this ages well) on TikTok is called "We listen, and we don't judge." Two people go back and forth confessing hilarious truths that the other did not know. As a therapist, my initial thoughts were, "Aw, this is so cute! Can we do this all the time, though? Like in real life?"

For kids who feel interrupted and experience being talked over, they simply shut down. Quite often, it seems that the car can be a safe place to have snippets of good conversations. No one must make eye contact, which feels less threatening. Kids would talk more if they believed they would be truly listened to. Full stop.

They want to be *known*.
"I wish they would see me more as a person than a thing you own."

Maisie, eleven, shared she had recently shown some interest in Harry Potter. She was frustrated, though, because her family kept reminding her that she did not like the series and that it scared her. Maisie told me in exasperation, "Yes, when I was *six*, it scared me, but don't they see I am older now and can like new things? It is like they have me forever locked into what was a much younger me!"

Because childhood is so fast and also takes forever to complete (depending on the perspective), there will be so many constant changes that it is hard to keep up. As adults our shifts don't happen with the same intensity and frequency as those of school-age kids, and we can forget how they can be rapid-fire yet developmentally typical. A kid can leave for school with a Fortnite lunch bag and decide somewhere during the day, for whatever reason, that he just isn't as much into it anymore. Irritating? Absolutely. Normal? Indeed.

One of my clients, Sloane, fifteen, likes to go on as she calls "long-winded rants" in sessions about her very specific special interest. If someone was listening in (rude) to our sessions in the middle of one of these tirades, they might wonder if "therapy was even happening." But Sloane would be quick to tell you that no one in her life will listen to her talk . . . about much of anything. Not just needing to end the conversation quickly; we are talking being unwilling to engage at all, because the topic is always considered "quite boring." Having an adult be fully present with her concerning something she is heavily interested in helps her to talk about her *actual* mental health challenges. Spoken struggles interspersed with the random titrates the intensity. Once pain can be expressed, a little more pressure is automatically released from her emotional safety valve. It's about balance, really.

They want *us* to be secure.

"My mom is amazing. I just wish she could know that, because she never thinks she is good enough for us. It makes me really sad."

Being comfortable in our own skin is a lifelong process, and we know kids are always watching. The process of liking ourselves has a ripple effect on those around us and is a lifelong journey. This takes more than affirmations every other day and a self-help book here and there. Both of those can contribute, but doing the inner work is what leads us to solid ground. Every decision we make to heal some aspect of ourselves, from a therapy session to a journal entry to a deep conversation with a friend about our real challenges, matters. Like deeply, truly matters.

Upon asking a kid/teen if I could share something with their parent that might be helpful, the responses vary. Having heard on more than one occasion "No!" the why received is often a similar response. "She will say, 'Well, I know that I am just the worst parent in the whole wide world, aren't I?' and we won't get anywhere." While not in those conversations, it sounds as if a layer of insecurity gets scratched, revealing defensiveness. It is hard for anyone to receive feedback, but if the anticipated response is a snapback, the likelihood of future constructive conversations is incredibly low. They are unlikely to try again in the same way to honestly communicate if it ended in a fight last time. To be fair, it is not fun to hear how we are (perceived to be) falling short, but I think that the sooner the lines of communication open in a relationship, the easier it is to set a foundation.

They want *us* to be authentically safe people.
"Don't tell me, 'You don't feel that way.' It makes me feel like you aren't really even listening."

While the word *safe* can be further unpacked to mean layers of things, it is my personal mission to continually transform into a safer version of myself. A general definition of a safe person is one with whom another individual feels comfortable sharing their thoughts and emotions without fear of judgment. So much of the time, we want to save people, naturally, from experiencing their pain. But the extra frustrating part is that we can't rescue them, and in attempting to do so, they feel more pushed under. They want us to be able to hold whatever they have to say, without feeling like we must fix it or make them land on the happy side of the emotions wheel.

They want us to continue to hold boundaries, communicate clearly, and offer grace as much as possible.
"My dad told us there is nothing we couldn't solve together, and that made me feel like no matter how bad I screwed up, there was some hope, and I wasn't going to be left alone."

"When they say they want to hear my side after a teacher calls them, it makes me feel like they actually want to hear what I have to say."

"When she follows through with the consequences she said would happen, it makes me frustrated, but I know that no matter what, those are the rules. I wouldn't respect her as much if she didn't enforce the boundaries she set herself."

Taking the conversation further, some of my friends (who were all former children) had some things to say too.

We needed to be understood.
"My dad never really 'got me,'" one of my friends shared. "He always wanted boys, and I was very much a girly girl. I always felt like he avoided me, because he didn't know what to do with me."

This happens often, where a kid will be really into an anime show (like, really into it) and no one speaks the language of their interest. While it is unnecessary to do a deep dive into Naruto, it doesn't hurt to ask curious questions to build a bridge. It isn't expected or even warranted for everyone to know everything, but if our aim is to really *get* our kids, the more we are curious about what they are moving through, the better chance we have of connecting with them on a deeper level.

We needed to be validated.
From the depths of me, I will never understand my mom's violent reaction toward me regarding molestation. How do you react like that toward a toddler and then throw them back into the lions' den? I've had dreams of a healthy reaction, which would be a response similar to any amazing mom in my life. She would look me in the eyes and say how deeply sorry she was that this thing happened, and she will do everything to keep me safe in the future. Something like that. The polar opposite response would have changed everything, and it is constantly on my radar to make sure glaring things are not missed. Had someone validated my pain then, the emotional plaque buildup in my heart would not be as thick as it is now. (Melissa has job security, just saying.)

What if our kids developed an inner voice that mirrored the validation in our own? What if, instead of an instant "Why did you do that?!?! You are the worst ever" when a kid made an easy mistake, she thought, *Oops. Need to fix that. I'll do better next time*, as a default response? What if the validation was wired into them so deeply that the kind voice reigned supreme? What a world.

Over dinner one night, I was expressing to my dear friend Dawn about not feeling *enough* with a complicated situation. She looked at me and said, "Did you say you *just* held space? You *just* held space? Like that isn't *everything*?" Whatever, Dawn.

We needed to be nurtured, not neglected, and held with compassion and respect.
My preferred bag, beloved #26, felt the fury of my rage unleashed during a kickboxing class with Big Feelings. Holidays stir things up for many, current company included. Did I need to be praised for my grades, or behavior, or speech and debate talents? Sure, but nowhere close to the deep desire to be held and comforted post my traumatic experiences. The year spent in Utah wreaked absolute havoc on my spirit, in ways my adult self is still learning to come to terms with. Slowly healing from the damage takes time, and it is not lost on me that had home been a safe place to be, my story would have taken an unrecognizable turn for the better.

But it didn't. I have lived my entire adult life without parents, so it will forever be a mystery how my mom and I would have communicated about my childhood. The alternate timeline where she lived comes with the awareness that to have any chance at real connection, I would have had to speak honestly. To not address the darkness of my childhood would leave no room for a real relationship. And to be honest, it is more likely that I would have distanced myself from her, as there is far too much ground to cover and not enough time.

I watch my adult friends with living parents, who either directly dealt them trauma or did not properly shield them from abuse in their childhoods, as they try to renegotiate the boundaries of their relationships. Those with a parent who was abusive are navigating the jungle of emotions associated with a person with whom they still interact. Dealing with an abusive parent who died means there is no longer chance for resolution, but also no more opportunities for uncomfortable conversations. However, the difference in now being an adult in relationship with parents is that while in childhood, they had little to no power to speak out.

With Love from a Children's Therapist

When we have a voice, everything changes. Which is exactly why I want to empower our children now—so that in twenty years, we don't learn they felt unheard.

Being so passionate about healing familial relationships where children are involved comes from knowing that one day they will be old enough to reflect through adult eyes. If the nurturing did not happen when it needed to, it simply becomes too late. Does this mean all hope is lost? No. But it is better to heal the neglect wounds in childhood than attempt to repair abusive damage as an adult.

Here is where I add an additional plea for the high-performing, well-behaved, seemingly well-adjusted kids. Over the years, *siblings* of a kid who is the identified client in the family have often been brought to me for extra support. Words fall short to show respect for that level of awareness in parents, in being proactive for the less squeaky wheel. Leo, six, has a brother who has high levels of need and has been known to show aggression toward many. He was explaining to me about a tantrum his brother had. Knowing about the show *Bluey*, thanks in part to my honorary three-year-old niece, Ada, I said, "It sounds like your brother is kind of like Jack [ADHD-representing dog] in *Bluey*?" He looked at me with huge solemn eyes. "Yeth. That is exactly what it is like. Like Jack." (Thanks, Ada!)

Truly, though, the kids/teens who are, for all intents and purposes, shiny on the outside, deserve checking in on as well. Sophie, twenty-four, saw me as a teenager and returned to process recent events. She expressed how her two siblings were having difficult times in their lives, and so all the air in the room was sucked out taking care of their needs. Neither parent had energy to check in on her, and she told me that she didn't even know how to talk about her life, because her problems seemed comparatively trivial. While there are seasons for everyone of intensity, please remember that the kids who are not outwardly screaming could be inwardly whimpering.

In my waiting room, three framed Charles Mackesy prints hang on the walls. Mackesy prints from his *The Boy, the Mole, the Fox and the Horse* collection are my absolute favorite, as they all carry a profound message in a simple way, with an accompanied beautiful sketch. His themes are about asking for help and forgiveness of ourselves and others. One about storms always ending catches my eye every day, as does the one above my door that talks about depression lying. Regarding "What Kids Wish Grown-ups Knew," his quote that best represents ending this chapter on a high note reminds us that we can all be lost and we can all be found:

"Sometimes I feel lost," said the boy.
"Me too," said the mole, "but we love you, and love brings you home."

#fromtheotherside

17

#lastvegasnerve

ULTRA-NEON DYSREGULATION

The attempt to escape from pain is what creates more pain. It is impossible to understand addiction without asking what relief the addict finds, or hopes to find, in the drug or the addictive behavior.
—Gabor Maté

HOURS AFTER MOVING INTO MY dorm at Arizona State, my first significant obstacle presented itself: walking into the new grocery store. The near silence and soft buzz of conversations were so incredibly . . . loud? What is this? No slot machines completely lining the entrance walkway, clanging with coins falling and noises emerging? What do you mean, *all* the stores close at night? Born and raised in Las Vegas, Nevada (not my choice, not my fault), apparently came with some quirky assumptions, not generally shared by the rest of the nation.

Naturally, at sixteen my first job was making balloon animals in restaurants for (*mostly,* *cough*) kids. A balloon artist, if you will. Having a job as a teenager based on *only* tips makes sense when half your city truly understands making a living on gratuity. Making interlocking heart hats at a reception for a newly married couple at Hippo and the Wild Bunch

Ultra-Neon Dysregulation

sounds like a super typical Thursday night for a high school junior, right?

While sure, our downtown was, you know, The Strip, living in the suburbs was honestly just like any other neighborhood. With lots of intense color everywhere you looked, that is. And main roads named Flamingo Avenue and Tropicana Drive. And with your high school AP Statistics class *entirely* centered around the art of gambling, addictive likelihood, and betting odds on casino games. Normal, nothing to see here.

Having now lived elsewhere, seeing actual stars in the sky *still* makes me smile. Colorado skies take my breath away, in a boundary-honoring way, though. The artificial sky ceiling at Caesar's Palace just never really hit the spot. The amount of neon signage reflecting in Vegas makes it nearly impossible to see constellations or the night sky clearly. The flashy lights crowd out everything else. Briefly returning to Vegas after my mom died was sensory overload, and my nervous system absolutely did not approve. Gambling in general stresses me out and reminds me of how many of my friends' parents growing up were lured by the siren song of the craps tables. Treating addiction, in my opinion, has many parallels to the allure of a roaring town built on entertainment.

One of the ways our kids are getting sucked in is the appeal of the flashy.

In my experience with addiction, both treating as well as having my own, other options must be louder than the fluorescent appeal of danger. This generation's youth are being targeted in numerous ways that set a foundation for addiction to flourish.

Vaping, for instance. (Picture red angry emoji here.) Vaping, the inhaling of an electronic cigarette, containing nicotine, other harmful chemicals, and flavorings, is as commonplace with our youth as their cell phones. The nicotine in one vape can be equivalent to the nicotine in fifty cigarettes. Teens will tell me how a parent confiscated a found vape pen, but a replacement is easily acquired. Mallory, sixteen, told me her mom threw away five of her vapes within a month, and she just found it to be comical. "As if I can't just get another one easily? Please."

While it is not new for companies to prey on children, the vape pen marketing teams know *exactly* what they are doing. Rainbow Sherbert, Chocolate Soda, and Berry Bomb Pop flavors? Ugh. There is already research on the impact of vaping, but twenty years from now, it is terrifying to think about the lungs of those addicted at thirteen. Kiera, fourteen, shared with me that the Banana flavor was gross, though, and she could promise she would never try *that one* again. Asking her what she would do if she wasn't able to vape was met with slowly blinking eyes and a confused emoji posture. She said, "Uh, I *will* always be able to, though. Everyone has one? I would just take a hit off someone else's pen" (implied *duh*).

Teen smoking is obviously not new, as a quick view of the 1978 *Grease* movie promo can confirm. However, what is unique to kids of today is the amount of appeal and normalizing of vaping in their culture. Kids tell me they vape with the pen up their sleeve in class, discreetly blowing out the smoke when a teacher isn't looking. Security guards are often outside school bathrooms, but kids say they find ways to hide and mask the smell. Addiction finds a way—and our kids are pretty addicted.

My maternal grandmother died of lung cancer when I was ten, so the appeal of smoking never captured me. Seeing her continue her habit, attached to machines keeping her alive (hello, 1989) was enough to deter anyone. But our kids need more evidence that these attempts to regulate their

Ultra-Neon Dysregulation

nervous systems are just a bait and switch to *way* bigger future problems.

The vagus nerve, not to be confused with Las *Vegas*, is the longest cranial nerve in the body, and it plays a key role in our mental health, including mood regulation and stress response. When *dysregulation* is mentioned, the vagus nerve has the starring role. Dysregulation is a state when we are having a challenging time managing emotions and/or disproportional reactions to situations. And since we were all toddlers once, my guess is that we all have at least some experience with feeling dysregulated. (No intentional shade to all you toddlers out there.) Helping our kids learn ways to manage their stress and calm their bodies can make the desire to look *outside themselves* less appealing.

In the final—as in "the night before it was due to the editors"—stage of this book, Microsoft Word on my computer completely malfunctioned, to the point where the words literally could not be accessed. All my knowledge about nervous system regulation became critically important in order to make my next moves. Reminding myself of safety mantras, seeking support from my dear friend Sherrey, using crackle wood in the fireplace, grabbing my stress ball and tossing it from hand to hand, enforcing mandatory snuggle time with my puppy, mindfully consuming a cold drink, wrapping myself in a fuzzy blanket, and breathing out all the air in my lungs were all strategies I intentionally practiced to be able to take my next steps. And since the book now exists again, logic came back online and we figured it out! Super rude timing, though, Word.

That incident can now serve as an example of how we in fact have power in times when things feel out of our control, as polyvagal theory suggests. Polyvagal theory is the collection of ideas about the vagus nerve's role in regulating emotions, social connections, and fear responses. Dr. Steven Porges, founder of polyvagal theory, states, "The body is resilient, and can handle long periods of pressure. But we need time to turn off, to relax. It's the ability to recover that many people have been robbed of, and our physical and mental health suffers. How safe we feel is crucial to our mental and physical health, and our happiness."[31]

We need to help our kids feel safe within and not be distracted by the neon carrot of addiction.

The addiction to technology and social media is blaringly loud, and our youth are listening.

Video games are a loaded topic, especially for families with a lot of related divisions. To me, the appropriate amount of screen time should be specific to each individual. If a child/teen is unable to sleep, achieve at their known standard at school, is defiant/rude afterward, those all play significant factors in determining the appropriate amount he or she should be allowed. Roblox, Fortnite, Minecraft, Zelda, Animal Crossing, Mario Cart, and Life Is Strange are games mentioned every day in my office, so my knowledge is decent related to their content. Problem solving, conflict resolution, teamwork, emotion regulation, and distress tolerance can all be positively impacted by participation, yet, of course, too much of a good thing is rarely a fantastic idea.

Ultra-Neon Dysregulation

Parents have shared that the issue begins when time is up and things become volatile in separating the child from the game. Here is where it becomes evident that it is addictive, as the descriptions often given to me mirror withdrawal.

The lure of games is so powerful and becoming even more so with their increased graphic abilities. I remain a fan of limited screen time, with clear boundaries, so as to create balance and not addictive tendencies. Saylor, fifteen, was not sleeping, going to school, or even regularly eating because she was absolutely addicted to her video game. Her mom felt at a loss, because she couldn't physically make her go to school or make her take care of herself. She felt afraid, especially due to her recent divorce, that Saylor's mental health was predicated on her ability to get lost in the game.

Saylor, a client prior to her addiction beginning, agreed to step away from the console for therapy sessions. We talked about appealing options outside the game world. *Of course* she wanted to get lost in the Zelda universe—her real one was chaotic and unpredictable. We planned for her to spend a reduced amount of time playing each day and replace it with something from the other list. Getting outside, starting a hobby, talking to a friend—these are fairly simple, nonthreatening options to create more space from the game. Could her mom have taken away the game in the middle of the night and destroyed or hidden it? Sure. But the likelihood of the addictive behavior transferring to something else equally detrimental would be high. Helping take away the flashy goodness of the Xbox and offering another bright yet potentially less intense option made Saylor choose for herself less Zelda, more real world.

Social media. Most people would say that they use at least one platform, and others would say several. We rely on these methods communication and connection to help facilitate daily living. Every teenager in my world uses Snapchat, and it comes up in conversation every single day. Knowing more than necessary about the app, my clients tell me story after story with Snapchat as the conduit in the plot. One of the features that gets on my nerves are "streaks." If you are not familiar, Snapchat streaks indicate that there has been consecutive communication with a person on their friends list for at least three consecutive days. Sure, it is fun to see constant communication with a best friend for the past seventy-one days. Neat. But when kids must be hospitalized for suicidality, the number one thing asked about is how to manage their streaks with people. "But who is going to keep up my streaks?!" Wish I was kidding.

Teens show me how they monitor everything from Snap Maps (let's see where every friend is at all times; *that* seems drama free) to when a message was read or seen compared to when a person was online. They will monitor who is highest on their friends list compared to another person and try to guess how into them another person is based on online activity. They will post passive-aggressive messages in their stories, intended to speak to a person, group, or couple. They will intentionally leave someone on read or delivered, to send a message of apathy. While teenage behavior was questionable prior to social media, handing a person without a fully developed frontal lobe access to so.much.data. is bound to come with some consequences.

None of the online sites are inherently bad; it is just important to ask questions and remain curious. Teens connect to their friends and find support and community online. But because it is so alluring to lose track of time chasing down

Ultra-Neon Dysregulation

someone else's online activity, it is important that we are aware of *what they are doing* with their screen time. The kids who do not have a phone or social media around the same time as their peers are dealing with different challenges, namely feeling left out. So much of the time, those kids tell me how aware they are about missing out on the drama.

Professionally, technology has proven helpful in so many ways. Phone activity comes with receipts, so teens read to me exactly what happened in a conversation or argument. Incredibly helpful in narrowing down what *exactly* happened. But the flip side is that the words, captured right there on the screen, can also be overanalyzed in a way that is detrimental. Bottom line is balance, and if we can step away from the phone/social media/website for a significant amount of time, it loses the vise-grip impact. In addition, technology helps our kids to feel safe in situations where they may need to contact others immediately. When events happen that make us all, not only the kids, feel unsafe, it can provide comfort to know that our people are easily accessible at a moment's notice.

The fear of school shootings dysregulates our kids without them even being fully aware. Never has growing up been devoid of challenges, yet these days there is so much more available to dysregulate kids. School shootings were never on my educational radar, as I was in college when the Columbine massacre occurred. The kids going to school today have never known a world where school shooters didn't exist, where they didn't need to know how to be quiet for an hour with a lollipop during a lockdown.

Paige, fifteen, curled up in my papasan and sighed deeply. One of my two offices, Twilight, with the chill vibe and twinkling lights, is often the choice for my teen/young adult clients. I was thankful for the ambience that day, as it had been a rough one for her. "We had an active shooter drill this morning," she murmured. "At lunch my friends and I were talking about what class we would want to be in when it happens. And what classes we would definitely be killed in because there aren't good places to hide. We should be talking about our *crushes* at lunch. Not this shit." She's not wrong.

Nolan, seven, entered my Sunshine room (think therapeutic Disneyland) with his head hung low. He had received light-up sneakers for his recent birthday and was not allowed to wear them to school. Nolan's teacher informed his parents that the flashing lights would compromise his safety in a school shooting. He wanted to talk about how afraid he was of being murdered before he lost all of his teeth. The Tooth Fairy wouldn't come if he died, and that would make him so sad.

Hearing the experiences of American kids going to school in a period where lockdowns are as commonplace as pop quizzes is simply heartbreaking. While this is a political issue, it is important to hold awareness that going to school can be fear producing for some, with good reason. Look, I work very hard, but there is no resolving that kids live in this world with actual people and in bodies and minds that don't always do what we want them to. There is nothing to tell them about this issue that fully satisfies. There just isn't. The very best we can do is offer guidance to be *connected to themselves* in the midst of whatever is swirling around them. Because when our brains are fully online and we are regulated, we can make the best decision available to keep ourselves as safe as possible.

Ultra-Neon Dysregulation

This doesn't mean we are devoid of emotion; it just means our emotions won't be running the show.

When my capacity to regulate my emotions was compromised trying to complete this project, I knew it was time to seek additional therapeutic support. Helping kids, teens, and young adults live in the same world with drugs, technology, and violence means staying committed to the end game. All these issues that exacerbate anxiety, depression, and addiction do not have to be black marks on mental report cards.

Glennon Doyle, author of *Untamed* and wisdom speaker, writes about mental illness and addiction. She states, "I've got these conditions—anxiety, depression, addiction—and they almost killed me. But they are also my superpowers. The sensitivity that led me to addiction is the same sensitivity that makes me a really good artist. The anxiety that makes it difficult to exist in a world where so many people are in so much pain—and that makes me a relentless activist. The fire that burned me up for the first half of my life is the exact same fire I'm now using to light up the world."[32]

We exist in a world full of noise and chaos, bright neon lights and pitch-black darkness. The very best we can offer our kids (and ourselves) is the ability to look for the signs of life up ahead. Maybe neon doesn't have to be *obnoxious*; maybe it can illuminate hope that we have been overlooking. Meanwhile, I'm waving over here in my little corner of the world, committed to helping our youth light up the world—*instead* of a vape pen.

#lastvegasnerve

18

#notmymothersbody
BODY-SHAMING CULTURE VIBES

*I definitely have body issues, but everybody does.
When you come to the realization that everybody does—
even the people that I consider flawless—then you can start
to live with the way you are.*
—Taylor Swift

THE ULTIMATE FANTASY MY ELEVEN-YEAR-OLD self was *mostly* convinced of was that if I stopped eating altogether, *maybe* eventually I could just sort of dissolve. Or at the very least, cease to function? In Utah, my heinous abusers withheld food quite often as punishment for entirely fabricated crime accusations. Naturally, my body, deprived of nutrition, started to shrink. Teaching myself how not to be hungry became a sport (because, screw them), and I consistently played varsity. My belief: it was my ticket out. Narrator: "While somewhat clever, this strategy was entirely ineffective. But her brain *felt* incredibly powerful and totally in charge. So, there's that." Therein lies the entire paradox of disordered eating: "I may not be in control of anything else, but I *am* in control of my body."

Eating disorders in many forms thrive in secrecy until it becomes obvious there is a problem. Every client who has shared with me their eating struggles began their restricted behavior quietly. No one knew until the problem became too loud to keep under wraps. Annabelle, fifteen, tried to confide in her mom about a pattern of disordered challenges with food, yet the response received was that she *looked* "healthy enough" so she must be fine. "Do I have to look like I am freaking starving to death for her to care that I need help?" she sobbed.

Sadie, twenty, felt self-conscious after gaining some weight in college out of state. In addition, she had developed crippling depression and had a dramatic fallout with her main friend group. Naturally, when she came back on summer break, there was a lot to talk about. As Sadie flopped onto my couch, she sighed, "Do you know the very *first* thing my mom said to me when I came home? 'Do you want us to pay for Ozempic?' Not 'I see your GPA dropped,' 'You seem really sad,' or 'You are not hanging out with your best friend anymore,' but 'You look fat.'"

Josh, fifteen, presents as a self-described "large kid," one who is genuinely feared on the football field. His dad told him he would "draw in more girls if he lost a couple of pounds and showed some abs." Naturally, this advice landed as discouraging to him, and he subsequently proceeded to eat even more junk food, as an intentional act of rebellion.

Vanessa, twenty-three, struggles with binge eating and feels shame that no one else knows when she has manic episodes in the pantry. Her mom, also dealing with obsessive thoughts about food, will not allow herself a full meal if she has not run enough that morning. Vanessa said, "If my mom, who is a walking skeleton, thinks she is overweight, what does she really think about *me*?"

Finley, eight, skipped up to me in the waiting room and promptly announced she was fat. Her mom gaped, "What did you just say?" Looking behind her shoulder, she replied, "Uh, what? I said that because you always say that too." Young girls (sometimes boys, but not as often) and teenagers saying over and over and over how much they hate their bodies often begins so early.

Disclaimer: the intention here is *not* to bash or shame moms (or other adults) for these messages. In fact, the prevalence of remembering the words of our significant caregivers is indicative that it has not been an uncommon experience. We come by it honestly; body acceptance and body positivity are newer concepts, thankfully gaining momentum. Awareness of the past informs future stories, and it helps to remember it is *both* what we say and what we do. These are simply examples of not only how powerful our words are to our kids but also how we communicate about *our own bodies*.

We all want healthy, thriving kids, *and* the language we use to talk about our bodies really matters.

Said with zero hesitation: *my* mom would absolutely *hate* the current representation of *my* body.

Even though she died twenty-three years ago, her belief system concerning women with muscles ran deep. I had no clear understanding of her spirituality, political stance, or even most of her childhood story, but you better believe that her belief about women's bodies was deeply ingrained—it is unattractive and not feminine for females to have visible muscles.

As an active kickboxer, my biceps have developed some visible definition. Seeing a picture of myself on a surfboard, arms out and muscles showing, my mom's voice resonated loudly in my head. *Women are* not *supposed to look like this.*

Disgusting. Over two decades without hearing her actual voice, and yet my *very first thought* was that my mom would undoubtedly respond negatively. The default messages from our parents run deep.

When the movie *Encanto* came out in 2021, my favorite character, Luisa, shined as an incredibly physically (and emotionally) strong female. Her song, "Surface Pressure," is my all-time Disney favorite. Her portrayal challenged traditional gender roles and showed a challenge to traditional femininity. Her song is about not feeling worthy, if she cannot be of service—which comes up in sessions with the oldest children in families, those considered "helpers," and kids who everyone views as "perfect." It was a validating anthem both to those who feel like they're carrying the world on their shoulders and to student athletes, proud of their strengths and abilities. Needless to say, I adore *Encanto*. In fact, a sign in my office reads "In *this* house, we talk about Bruno."

Luisa's strength is also a great launching pad for conversations with kids about what their bodies can *do*, not just how they look. One of the ways to take back the power in the food conversation is the reminder that there is no moral value to food. It is simply fuel. Educating kids on what makes their bodies feel better gets way more mileage than shaming about serving sizes. Because yes, we want our kids to make informed choices about food; however, it does seem to be more effective when the conversation doesn't take place right when the bite is literally happening. Sure, they might put a few fries back, but at what cost? Improved longer-term nutritional choices are built from a series of conversations, not awkward moments in front of others.

Charlotte, fifteen, suffers from ARFID (avoidant/restrictive food intake disorder). More than simple "picky eating," people with ARFID have legitimate fears of food and sensory challenges that make it extremely difficult to consume food. Charlotte's mom joined us in my office, and we talked about a manageable breakfast plan for the week. This is not Charlotte's primary issue, but one causing disruption, so we have been working through managing her anxiety around food. Her mom, wanting her daughter to eat anything, recognizes it is not about coercion, but rather, it's about understanding the deeper issues behind the eating disorder. Many teenagers share being secretive about eating habits, because out-loud conversations with grown-ups typically do not end well. To understand where a kid/teen comes from regarding eating habits is the bottom line, name of the game. When we understand motivation *behind* behavior instead of only looking at their plates, we are more equipped to have conversations that matter.

Messages about our weight, food, and body image all run deep. One of my friends shared she can still recall her mom treating her and her sister differently, especially when it came to cookie distribution, and another remembered her mom being continually deeply critical of other women's weight. Others remember their mom's expressing jealousy about their daughter's body and reminiscing about being a similar size. We remember moments from childhood when our body was objectified. When parents help kids learn actual names of body parts early, this can help prevent abuse and improve honest communication.

Body shaming; criticizing yourself or another about their appearance, has gotten a lot of attention in recent years. Kids today are more aware of this concept than perhaps generations before and are developing a keen radar to detect passive-aggressive body comments a mile away. Many a child has commented on how fast my puppy, Willow, is growing, and responding to the tune of "Hey, don't body shame my dog" has gotten a laugh as well as started a relevant conversation about the topic. (Not my first rodeo.)

Ivy, eighteen, *was* proud after posting her senior pictures online, until an aunt messaged her about her (gasp) cleavage. It completely rained on her parade. The pictures could not have been more appropriate, yet it is clear she has developed into a woman (as one does.) The damage was already done, though, and despite sharing with Ivy that the portraits looked amazing, it was too late. To remove the sound bites of negative interactions takes time and intention, and sometimes it becomes a long-lasting part of mental noise.

That's what we're trying to do our best to prevent.

Honestly, though, we live in a fully image-obsessed world. Look around: damaging messages about the value of "perfect" bodies are everywhere and never stop. Thousands of products to enhance any perceived visual flaw are readily available. And whatever creepy algorithm listens and watches, they somehow know our insecurities and advertise accordingly. Taytum, twelve, shared that not looking like her favorite YouTuber "made her feel so bad about herself," so she jumped at the chance to buy the skin care that said influencer suddenly began to market. I asked her to think, *Who profits off this emotion?* regarding her mood shift via the content creator. This is another reason why it is important to know who is grabbing their attention during screen time and from pop culture in general. Teens will share that a TikToker they follow has had success on a fad diet, so they might as well give it a try—because our kids are susceptible to following the advice of fellow young people over that of a significant adult in their lives.

A popular movie actress was recently all over the news with accusations of being "dangerously thin." When her movie came out, numerous tween/teen clients brought the subject up and asked my opinion. While we can make guesses, it seems unfair to draw conclusions that cannot be backed in the moment. As fans and not friends of the actress, we talked about how we don't really know what is going on behind the scenes. These are important conversations to have; we only know the full story if we in fact know the full story.

Don't get me started on dress codes either, which are seemingly mainly created for the female population. Not that it doesn't happen, but never has a male client told me they were dress coded at school. Typically, it is about shirts that don't cover leggings, showing shoulders (gasp), or revealing skin around belly buttons. Sometimes when the subject comes up, I share that since many years ago ankles were considered scandalous, my prediction is future generations will look at us the same way about shoulders. Years ago, a twelve-year-old client decided that the dress code at her middle school was sexist, so she was going to fight back. She rallied several of her friends, and they bravely approached the principal. "Your rules, that I am distracting boys by my clothes, makes me feel bad about myself for no reason. We want it to be changed to be fair." To his credit, the girls were listened to, and the school abolished significant portions of the dress code. Not every fashion choice needs to be highlighted, and when we allow kids to make choices making them feel safe in their bodies, everyone wins.

Bailey, eleven, shared that she never felt connected to the feminine ideal of girls and is often mistaken for a boy. She wishes that the gender binary conversation regarding feminine and masculine energy was different and that people didn't feel so entitled to make comments about her presentation. The principle of not commenting about a person's body with feedback they cannot change in five minutes or less has always been a strategy that makes sense to me, as I shared with her. You have something in your teeth, yes, mention it. Your hips look huge in those jeans, big NO.

One of my teenage clients asked me recently how often *I* weigh myself. She learned that the scale and I broke up long ago, and the lifelong goal is to try to love my body at every size. I told her things along the lines of how that stupid little machine once would dictate my self-perception for the day, and that landed for me as lame and unfair. The scale and sometimes even the mirror are unreliable narrators. From my perspective, the scale has had a toxic impact on the collective body image of our youth. But what is important to me, as an adult speaking into their lives, is that the responsibility to model body confidence is always in my court.

Another way self-image issues with our youth manifest is wanting to be physically separate from their bodies. Piper, seventeen, shared that she was persuaded by a boy to go further sexually than she had wanted to. Desperately wishing for him to like her and not wanting to seem immature created a perfect storm of inevitable regret. Piper proclaimed, "I wish I could just unzip my skin and leave my body behind. One that has never been touched in icky ways that make me gag thinking about it." She tried to share these feelings with her mom, and in a misguided but genuine attempt, her mom said just to move on to the next boy. Let me be very clear: when we are traumatically forced to leave our bodies, returning home is only through the (painful) path of intentional healing.

Hazel, fourteen, stopped eating after a significantly tragic event in her family. Instead of forcing her to consume meals, we worked together on ways she could feel stronger apart from food. She discovered Krav Maga, a self-defense martial arts technique gaining popularity. Instead of focusing on the fact she was not eating enough, we talked about the nutrition it would take in order to be the most effective at her new sport.

Hazel came to conclusions on her own about protein and the necessity of increasing her intake to take down the boys in her class (which was an extra surprise bonus).

Kids/teens/young adults recovering from trauma deserve tender loving care dealing with their body images.

Let's help kids grow up in a world where they don't believe they need to shrink themselves, literally or figuratively, to be safe, protected, and loved. In addition, my mom might not have ever appreciated my muscles, but *I* do. Every day, my goal is stronger, not smaller, and empowerment over vanishing, please. At the end of the day, my hope for all of us is the reminder that we are the only ones who ever fully live in our bodies. Even our mothers don't get to live there.

#notmymothersbody

19

#preapproved
APPROVAL ADDICTION

*I wish I could show you when you are lonely or in darkness
the astonishing light of your own being.*
—Hafiz

AT THE TOP OF THE *Things I Wish I Had Known Sooner* checklist: your main objective in life is *not* to make sure everyone likes you. Wait, what? Undoubtedly, my inaugural mission on this planet was to figure out exactly how to be the missing piece everyone needed. Born and raised as a competitive people pleaser, the implied lesson came early: it just wasn't acceptable or safe to be *authentically* myself.

I constantly received this message both directly and covertly:

Don't show that you are too smart; no one likes a know-it-all. Don't talk too much, or too loud, or too anything. Don't ever mention anything you are good at; it's obnoxious. Make sure you are never first in line or take the last of anything. Don't even show that you care about the line, for that matter. And for the love of God, definitely never spill, break, ruin, or lose anything.

Becoming a watered-down version of myself, who was *not too much* or *not enough*, was the name of the game. When we grow up spending too much time focusing on how to make everyone *else* comfortable, it leaves us feeling internally at odds. Many kids tell me they struggle with naming their positive traits, because it feels like bragging. But ask them to point out their perceived flaws and a long, itemized inventory suddenly appears. Looking at merchandise these days, it appears that *many* need the message "I am more than enough." If everywhere you turn a magnet or hoodie can be purchased with the reminder, missing core messages from childhood are likely to play a key role.

Juxtapose this concept with kids who deeply believe they will be loved and approved of no matter what, and you'll find a world of difference. Gracie, eleven, homeschooled and heavily involved in sports and family activities, deals with anxiety unrelated to her status in this world. Her language indicates she is mostly unaware of the social pressures other tweens are experiencing. Gracie carries herself with confidence born from deep security. While she has plenty of *other* challenges, she doesn't have any desire to go against her convictions. Gracie is more inoculated from peer pressure and has no tolerance to entertain anything that doesn't feel right. This is due to intentional and deliberate efforts of her parents to build her up and to teach her that her value does not come from other people. It makes me wonder, *What if we sent all of our kids into the world already believing they were preapproved?*

Kids and teens who feel *genuinely* supported at home have less of a need to seek outside approval.

For me, a solid Enneagram 2 (the Helper), approval addiction started young (In utero? Jury is still out). Twos, for example, often grow up in environments where they feel like their basic emotional needs are not met. Unhealthy home environments create an ability to adapt early on and repress needs—all to support others. While this adaptation isn't unique to only one personality type, being aware of the motivation behind behavior has always proven to be helpful. The dark side of helping, though, is to do so at the expense of ourselves, which can lead to resentment. (I also want to give a plug here to investigate the Enneagram test; it continues to be transformative for me as a human and a clinician.) As a 2, let me help you, geez.

Daphne, nineteen, shared a potential conflict in her upcoming new roommate/dorm situation for the Fall semester. Already knowing what she wanted, it required straightforward communication to solve. She asked for advice, so we talked through some potential dialogue. Her hesitancy to address it, though, became clear, and I told her, "The truth is that the current disagreement is not all on you. *However*, if you hold on to it, don't say anything, and then explode three months down the road, that then *is* your responsibility." Daphne, like many, is afraid of making anyone upset or creating waves. The bigger issue, I explained, is that problems like these don't just go away. They build up until a breaking point, and when we are screaming or passive-aggressively slamming doors by October, the approval we desire doesn't magically follow. As I told her, "Saying yes when you mean no only delays the annoyance, and then the problem is compounded." Plus, it is unfair to yourself and others not to be true to your word. As I often say to friends, "Your no helps me trust your yes."

While in Utah, one of my survival strategies was total compliance. Watching older girls fight back did not end well for them. Innocently, though, my younger self sadly believed compliance meant being complicit. Unwarranted shame happens when our body shuts down, and yet it likely saved my life to freeze. My body knew exactly what to do, and the desire to be submissive and not anger them further likely prevented horrific situations from escalating.

Now, with my power restored, self-regulation strategies are regularly managed at my beloved kickboxing studio, where visualization and safe (but loud) hooks contact the bag, and permission to go at maximum capacity is not required. It is where all that could not be fought against as a child can be fully raged out, with no concern for anyone's approval. That is, anyone who isn't the teaching instructor at that time. (We are a work in progress.)

Michelle, my favorite boxing instructor, also competes in Muay Thai, the full combat sport. "I punch bags so I don't punch people" is my standard line when asked about my stress management strategies. When she asked if I was coming to her first big fight, it tore me up inside to have to decline. "Sadly, no. I can't watch you get hit." Did I want to show up as a good friend? Obviously. Would attending potentially compromise my own mental health, with flashbacks of my own endured violence? Inevitably.

In the past, saying no would have caused pain and rumination for days. Likely, I would be saying things to myself to the tune of "Seriously? Just get over it. Holy rolled eyes emoji, Batman! She is choosing to be in this situation, and she is not in literal danger. Good Lord." (My inner voice has gotten *much* kinder, thankfully.)

After doing years of my own healing work, the reality is that on no level is it good for me to engage in that kind of situation. It would be visually detrimental, and the emotional cost would be too high. And even when asked by the studio owner later to attend, with his request of, "Stacy! We need your energy there!" My response was that I could not but would be happy to make cupcakes for the post event celebrations. (I'm known for making adorable things out of food, just ask my people.)

Young humans, however, do not have historical data if a situation would be harmful or not. Often kids/teens tell me choices were made simply because they did not want another person to be mad/sad/disappointed.

This is so relatable.

As an adult, "Absolutely not" is my response to *anything* horror related—movies, books, events, etc. (Real life is scary enough, thanks!) Not my jam. But when Halloween rolls around, kids/teens who honestly *also* don't enjoy being scared get invited to haunted houses. They don't want to go. We talk about ways to connect with friends to meet up after or come up with ideas to protect themselves from experiencing things they do not want to. When it comes to higher stakes, scenarios where drugs or other illegal activity is happening, we talk through the motivation to be there in the first place. I try to validate how hard it is to go against the grain, but how much more they will respect themselves when they do. Conversation centers around chasing authenticity, not approval.

It is in some of these hard social situations, too, that safe adults can use this time to shine. Having the ability to support a kid/teen when they are potentially in the paws of the peer pressure beast is a gift. One of my favorite older kid strategies with parents is the random emoji text. This starts with agreeing on a predetermined uncommon emoji between adult and kid that is a bit of a code word. The parent receiving the random emoji is translated as "Please pick me up, make up an excuse, get me out of this situation." Bonus if it *also* means no questions asked. Kids have shared with me they have gotten out of sexual situations, uncomfortable sleepover scenarios, criminal activity, and internal warning bells ringing with this plan. Sure, it would be great if we lived in a world where life was as simple as an after-school special. Or easily wrapped up in a single episode, for that matter. Helping our kids not have to accept every invitation means approaching situations with intention.

◈

A maladaptive way that kids/teens are learning from their peers how to cope with their emotions is via self-harm. Up to this point, there have been hundreds of kids who've walked through my door having some form of self-inflicted burn, cut, or damage to their skin. Self-harm is an addiction, and according to the American Psychological Association, it impacts at least 17 percent of the teenage population. I have disappointing news: self-harm bears the same reality as other addictions, that one must want to stop the behavior. As frustrating as it is to watch someone we love suffer with an addiction, it simply will not take if the teenager feels that the self-harm is serving them. The key is in finding the desire to even *want* to find a different way, before attempting to make them cease the behavior. Many alarmed parents learn of their child's cutting and will frantically beg me to make them stop. While my efforts are always in the best interest of the child, there are natural limitations to my ability. One shift important to helping our kids who cut could be less punishments resulting from the discovery of self-harm incidences. While consequences often result from of a sense of helplessness, the message sent is not an accurate one. To see the outcome of a self-harm episode is to witness the aftermath of a scream turned inward.

Self-harm, often listed now as NSSI (non-suicidal self-injury), can be a misguided attempt to manage pain. Those suffering will sometimes say that to see themselves bleed makes their emotional suffering less intense, as there is a different pain to focus on. Teens have told me that it makes their pain seem valid, as there is now actual evidence. There have been online forums that encourage NSSI teens to compare cuts and show the rest when they are struggling. (Thanks for that, toxic groups.) Instagram, however, officially changed its policies in 2020 to remove all graphic content related to self-harm, which was a game changer. Clients had consistently shared with me pride about their sobriety only to mindlessly scroll and stumble across a boasting self-harm image.

Mackenzie, twelve, explained that her self-harm arm scars, visible in a tank top, made her feel vulnerable. Her boyfriend's relative saw her marks as an open invitation to discuss her mental health. (Never is this a good idea.) As she told me to share here with people longing to do better, "Bringing more focus to it does not help." Whether or not a child/teen is "cutting for attention," it is problematic behavior. There is a deep wound already if they are harming their body to get some level of support. When kids feel seen without the need to take a lighter to their body, it can only positively impact their likelihood of recurrence.

Ginny and Georgia, a widely popular show among the teenage population, made it into my queue (for the kids.) Really, though, it shows a realistic portrayal of a teen struggling with self-harm. Ginny, fifteen, reveals first to her dad that she is burning herself and needs therapy. He vows to help find her support and thanks her for telling him. (The therapist scenes, though, helped my clients appreciate their own therapist, who tries her hardest to be sensitive and, you know, has a personality.) Yet when Georgia, her mom, finds out, her reaction to her daughter rapidly spirals from rage to despair to the most helpful response—compassion. Her mom says after first responding with anger, "I am so sorry I missed this. Give it to me. You give all that pain to me. I can handle it."[33]

Layla, fourteen, told me that had her mom responded like Georgia about her self-harm addiction, she would have sobbed with gratitude for days. Instead, her mom did not leave the anger portion of feelings and promptly grounded her for an incredibly long time. (Just so we are clear, again—this response is not helpful for anyone.)

While it makes sense to remove sharps, razors, knives as temptations as a response to self-harm discoveries, it is additionally important to show the teenager you will do anything to help. The I Am Sober app is utilized by many of my clients and helps them to record and celebrate sobriety from just about anything. The ones who are hesitant to use this tool, however, either do not want their parents to see it downloaded and have questions or fear their parents will learn there has been a relapse. Often, I guide my clients to change their body temperature when they are feeling activated to self-harm: holding an ice cube, running outside into the snow barefoot, drinking hot tea, taking a hot shower, etc.—to shock the system into a temporary re-set.

To show our teens that despite struggling with self-harm, they can come to us with anything burdening them does far more for their health than trying to police every moment. Because the reality is that if they want to find something to self-harm, they will. Most of all, there is literally nothing that can replicate your unconditional love toward someone who struggles.

Another observed way some teens/young adults desperately seek approval is through sexual activity. By no means is this a new phenomenon, yet it comes up quite often in my office. Katelyn, sixteen, speaking about her crush, indicated she'd be "unable to say no" to a potentially sexual situation. She really wanted a boy who was showing her, in my opinion, minimal attention and interest to choose her. "Stop handing over the keys to your self-worth to a boy who *literally* cannot drive yet," I told her. When I hear James Arthur's song "Empty Space," which talks about fruitlessly searching for love in a stranger's bed, my mind always drifts to clients over the years who were willing to silence their own internal alarm in exchange for perceived temporary approval from others.

During the 2020 COVID-19 pandemic, therapy sessions were conducted via telehealth, per state law. People were getting desperate for connection, and teens especially felt the impact of social separation. One of my clients, thirteen, shared that the only place her mom would let her go to see her friends was the local park. She chose to meet up with a boy, instead of her friends, and have sex in a park porta potty. Sharing this with me at her next session, we talked about self-respect and how that could look instead moving forward.

I asked her gentle questions about how that decision landed in her body, and if she thought maybe, just maybe, she deserved far more than what she settled for. She cried admitting she knew it was gross, but if she said no, the boy would move to the next on the list. I said in no uncertain terms, "Um, well, I would *hope* so. And you, my friend, should never feel like just a name or a number. What if you realized you should be cherished? What if you felt like you were worth more than your body? What if you were the one deciding whether to move on or not?" Chances are, as she continues down the road, she will (hopefully) continue to see herself as more valuable than the choices she made that summer day.

One of my favorite series from 2015, *The Unbreakable Kimmy Schmidt*, contains a line intended to be funny but lands for me as incredibly poignant. Matt Lauer's character says, "I am always amazed at what women will do because they're afraid of being rude."[34] Recently, a news scandal in my immediate area regarding sexual exploitation of children broke headlines. The severity of the abuse paralleled too much of my own story, and it was deeply upsetting. Knowing the ethics of not compromising one's own mental health, I sent a message to the school county admin, requesting my removal from the referral list of available crisis counselors. Because guilt consumed me regarding not having capacity to take on the traumatized clients, I reached out to my own therapist.

Melissa responded, "Kindness includes self and does what is best for all. Niceness excludes self and just pleases others. Screw being nice. Be kind."

Let's teach our kids/teens that self-respect will do far more for them than any unnecessary choice they could make. That they deserve to choose who touches their bodies, what they are willing to tolerate, and exactly what they have capacity to do. And that it is always in their best interest to make important decisions with feedback from someone they trust and respect.

And may they never choose a dirty bathroom to sell dignity for cheap approval. Ever.

Fun fact: I wear a shade of purple . . . every day. For the last several decades. Is it weird? Yes. Am I easy both to shop for and to find in a crowd? Also, yes. My belongings are generally purple, too, so if I leave something somewhere, it is easily returned. (You are welcome, everybody.) Purple feels safe and comforting to me, and quite literally, I don't care what people think about it. The other day, a lady in my work restroom commented, as we were washing our hands, "I love that you are always pretty in purple. How do you know when it is in season, though?" And I said with a smile, "Uh, I am just unbothered? Nobody gets to decide what I wear." (Insert apathetic shrug here.)

Wearing glasses as a little girl, there were some kids in elementary school who called me "four eyes." Even back then my thought was, *That is the laziest insult. Is that really your best material?* In eight-year-old speak, of course. But really, it didn't even impact me. Not because there was so much security at home, but because of my confidence in being much wittier than those fools. Now, had something valid been spoken (you read too much and *love* the library; eww, your mom washes tongues for a living; or you wish Levar Burton from *Reading Rainbow* was your dad), well, that may have been effective.

Regina George, however, is legit, though. For reference, the movie *Mean Girls* depicts a social food chain ruled by popular girls called the Plastics. Regina George is the head Queen bee—popular, manipulative, and powerful. The movie is hilarious, but accurate in many ways to modern-day school attendance. Asking any one of my female clients who the Regina is in their school, they can tell you in 2.4 seconds. *Mean Girls* is a great example of how a deep desire for approval motivates so much of teen behavior. And how it doesn't usually end for the better.

Not sure if you have read a preteen girl group chat lately where one person starts mad, but big yikes! So many conversation threads—over text, email, and social media—where the dialogue can best be described as . . . mean. Not saying that boys do not have the capability for the same type of interaction, but it does seem often to be female energy. We tell our kids to "not listen to them" and to "forget about it," which would be satisfactory strategies—if they consistently worked. The best we can do in these scenarios is to remind them that believing hurtful words is handing over our power to someone else. I explained to Declan, nine, "When you let the other kids call you a 'loser,' it is similar to what happens in your video game. You only get so many hearts, rights? And the more the monsters attack, you lose your heart bar power. There are things you can do to regain your health, but it takes time and money. When you get called names, and you start to let it impact your day, you are giving those little hearts away for free, *and also*, you have less energy to fight the battles you need to. Just saying."

There is not a way to fully protect our kids (or anyone, to be honest) from the words, actions, and choices of other children. Kids can be so mean, and that reality isn't changing any time soon. The anti-bullying campaigns at school at least call attention to the behaviors but can do little to curb the subtle jabs that happen all day long. Cyberbullying, which has gained awareness in the last decade, can be the most brutal when it comes to impacting self-esteem. In the '80s and '90s, kids who were experiencing bullying could just go home (and get bullied there, but that is a *separate* conversation). Kids/teens have been terrorized by fake accounts used to mock them, been spammed nonstop hate messages, other experienced kids hacking into their profiles and changing passwords, and the cruelest messages you could imagine. I've heard it all, and reading sometimes (most of the time) it is about a boy or some other person feeling jealous and insecure.

In my opinion, it does little in those moments to say, "Ignore them," because, how?

In my observation, the situations in the cyberbullying realm are much more subtle than the outright cruel words that can be posted on someone's TikTok, or via a direct message on Instagram. Much of the time, it looks more like a thirteen-year-old posting a Snapchat story with a group of girls, intentionally minus one and a caption reading "All my hot besties together—left no crumbs." It doesn't look like anything dark is happening—except to the one girl not invited from the tight friend group.

And this is not exclusive to girls: boys are sometimes left out of the Fortnite five p.m. group, not invited to the birthday party with all their friends, or not chosen for the team, yet all the pictures are promptly posted online. These aren't situations to police, because no one is inherently committing an offense. Annalise, thirteen, shared with me a Truth or Dare disaster from her last sleepover with her friends. Choosing Dare, Annalise's friend said, "Hand over your phone and let me search my name in your messages." Right? However, these are the moments when I encourage my clients to honestly evaluate traits they want in close friends. And also, to take a moment to look inward about the kind of friend they would like to be.

While it isn't always realistic to suddenly acquire a new friend group, it helps us consciously acknowledge and pay attention to what we deserve. Quality friendships take time, I often say to kids. But they are so worth it. You will find your people; maybe not tomorrow, but one day. Not every relationship has to be a close one, and when you are hurt, take note of what you liked and did not appreciate. Learn how *you* can be an even better friend, and don't put *all* your waking effort into getting others' approval. Be grateful that people who did not know how to compassionately hold you, lost their grip entirely. Focus on the people who *are* showing up for you, not the ones you long for. *You* need to like you, and that path is the most important of all. And if all else fails, respond like Ted Lasso, when asked if he believes in ghosts: "I do, but more importantly, I think they need to believe in themselves, you know?"

#preapproved

20

#hoperestored
BECAUSE REDEMPTION

Know that one day your pain will become your cure.
—Rumi

"MISS STACY? CAN I TELL you something? I, um, really don't want to live anymore," whispered my eight-year-old client, as she placed Elsa upstairs in the dollhouse. Sent as an urgent referral from Children's Hospital, she was considered immediate high risk. This small child emanated so much emotional pain, for reasons still to be determined.

"Thank you for telling me, and I am so, so glad you are here," I responded.

Looking up and peering through messy bangs, she said, "You are? But why?"

"Because *here* is *exactly* where *I* would have wanted to go when I was a little girl and didn't want to live anymore," I whispered back. "Can we figure out how to help you want to live again, together?"

Countless times in my childhood, utter and deep despair threatened to consume me. Depression felt like slogging through thick mud with unhelpful shoes—with no clear direction or hope. During significant portions of growing up, an adult me didn't seem probable, given the circumstances. (Look, little Stacy, we made it!)

Younger me wasn't given the guidance or support she needed to thrive (but her *teeth* are fabulous). Adult me has invested significant time, money, and energy into healing what was fractured as a child. Finding the parts that have been wounded, letting the suffering be heard, and getting the right support has forever changed my life. My therapist, Melissa, is gentle, yet relentless in not letting me minimize the pain. Or change the subject, but whatever. She has proven that we can face even the darkest of backstories, if we are held with compassionately safe hands.

Prentis Hemphill writes, "There's something revolutionary about creating a space for people to lay down what burdens them. Concealing this pain wears down our capacity for vulnerability and connection, and eventually our bodies, too."[35] Not to develop a lifetime of hiding but to live fully, whole, and free—this is the heartbeat of my career in helping kids on the front end of their lives.

Once upon a time, my intention was to brand my private practice "Hope Restored." However, the feedback from colleagues was that Stacy Schaffer is catchy enough and an easy-to-remember name. Now "hope restored" remains my Instagram handle and also embodies what I believe is possible about the human condition. Helping hurting kids heal comes from a place of deep inner knowing. Familiar with feeling all alone, scared, ashamed, and hopeless, it is my life's mission to help kids/teens/young adults breathe easier.

Currently, my six-month-old therapy puppy in training, Willow, is enrolled in private obedience classes. Honestly, the appointments fill me with pure dread. Not sure if Willow and

Because Redemption

I share the same experience (because treats), but for me, there are several things that could be chosen instead. Like trauma therapy, grueling chores, or boring taxes, for example.

Our trainer, Ms. Trunchbull, is clearly knowledgeable and experienced with dog obedience, no question. However, pets typically have owners attached to them, so one would hope that an additional skill set in working with people would develop over time. Since we purchased a package deal, we have the same trainer for the duration. Thankfully, the days are numbered. (Two left, but who is counting? I am. I am counting.) While it is (hopefully) not her intention, the sessions leave me feeling patronized, annoyed, and frustrated. Feeling small and chastised, I leave feeling doubtful about my abilities as a dog mom. At the core, this is the exact opposite set of feelings we are going for regarding people entering my practice or reading this book.

You are the expert on the kids/teens in your life.

Yes you are.

You know their quirks, their likes, their warning signs, their hopes, their dreams. While I have perhaps taken more child development classes than the average bear, my goal is simply to come alongside for extra support. Most of what I know is from on-the-job training. The role plays in graduate school were . . . nice, but none of them hit on what it is *really* like to be a children's therapist. It's intense. But the fact you picked up this book and made it this far (yay, you!) means there is an investment in the young person/people in your life. That alone should be celebrated.

Edited to note: the dog training company owner reached out after we ultimately decided *not* to continue with the remaining two sessions. She appropriately validated my concerns, apologized for not intervening sooner after seeing confusing training notes, and unconventionally connected us to a different trainer, who is absolutely wonderful. It's proof that honest communication can actually be effective. Something I'm continuing to learn. Who knew?

Parenting, teaching, existing are all challenging verbs in the act of living as a human being. While there is always so much to learn if we are trying to better understand ourselves and other people, we need to grant each of us some clemency in the process. My therapist gig is arguably easier than the harder job of parenting, in that the day-to-day intensity doesn't exist. I get to remind kids of the radiance inside them, and you get to watch them glow over the long haul.

Before my mom died, her wish was to see all the lighthouses in the United States. (In case you are wondering, to fourteen- and fifteen-year-old eyes, all lighthouses look exactly.the.same.) But there was something she loved about them, and living in a landlocked state, it felt necessary to her to travel several summers down the Pacific Northwest and the East Coast. A part of me wonders if there was something to the symbolism of finding direction when all else feels lost. Since her answers are never coming, my conclusion is that the lighthouse shows the absolute beauty of resilience despite all versions of turbulent waters. In my waiting room, a large canvas displays a lighthouse against a (mainly) purple sunset, which remains as a quiet tribute to my mom. The lighthouse serves as a reminder to continue to transform the twisted madness of my own childhood into a healing presence for kids still living in theirs.

It feels unclear how to *teach* resilience, because there has always been a fire burning inside me, fueled with determination. We all have an internal lighthouse, though, guiding us back to ourselves. When we *only* look *outside* ourselves for the answers, affirmations, or awareness, it is hard to clearly see the line of the shore. To tap into our internal reserves means to deeply connect to our own wisdom and sense of direction and find inward comfort. For all of us to safely reside within our own lighthouses, shining beacons from our own light is the message for us all. The Head and the Heart sings something to this effect in one of my favorite verses about being our own arrow and ultimately our own home. We can help brighten the path for our kids, our teens, and each other, but it is crucial to remember the origin story of the radiance within. We are born with light, and the work is to help one other find it when things get dark.

This is my exact wish not just for my young clients but for *all of us*. Secure, confident, and at-peace adults undeniably help forge a better world for the generations that follow. My hope is that you have found something within these chapters that resonates and can help illuminate your journey. As Lisa Dion eloquently states, "In a world that gives constant direction to children regarding who they should be, the greatest gift we can give children is to help point their compass inside themselves."[36] May the kids in your life—and the one who lives inside you—find safe and brave spaces to be heard, loved, valued, respected, and empowered—and never feel completely alone.

I'm learning I am not.

With Love,
A Children's Therapist

#hoperestored

APPENDIX

#withlove

CLOSING THOUGHTS

ON A SNOWY COLORADO EVENING the other night, conditions were perfect for staying indoors with a fireplace and a good book. Seeing as the weather was in the single digits, every client left our sessions mentioning something about staying warm. However, it was Tuesday—my favorite kickboxing night—so making the trek from my office through freezing weather was still a no-brainer.

Willow, my therapy puppy in training, will be eight months this week and is adored as the studio mascot. As I was scrambling with my literal wagon filled with all the gear needed to make these sessions happen, and wondering why this choice was made instead of fleecy pajamas, the answers became clear.

My kickboxing studio is one of the most important places where I belong—for my dog, my body, and my mental health.

Seeing we'd arrived, Kat and Ella rushed out from the front desk to get the door for us, Nick, the manager, exclaimed to first-time kickboxers, "That is our mascot!" and Michelle, our instructor for the night, calmed her excited furry niece with chest rubs before she taught our class. Alex, another instructor, came to gush over Willow, who always rolls over immediately for her. Then we passed the brand-new sign on

Closing Thoughts

our way farther into the studio that read, "Please wipe your snowy paws! :) *not just Willow."

My kickboxing friends played with her as I changed, someone filled up her water bottle, and Willow peacefully settled next to my punching bag with her bag of toys. She was completely unbothered by the loud music, punching sounds on bags, and the volume of instruction, since she has been coming since she was ten weeks old. My friends and I checked in with each other about life before class started, and someone grabbed a mat for me. One friend, EZ, came over when it was time for core work because Willow does not appreciate when I am on the ground and not playing with her (how rude). He wordlessly took her outside so I could do a sit-up or two. People came over to greet and pet her afterward, while telling her she is the very best part of coming to class. As I was leaving, someone mentioned how they were going to make a "Willow Wall" in the studio with pictures of her taken with various people. I guess you could say she is a regular.

Driving away through falling snow, I was moved to tears by how grateful I am to have this community. Not only for me but really for my puppy. Because this has been her life; she knows nothing other than being completely accepted and adored.

The reality stopped me in my tracks. I mean, not literally, because safety first, but still.

How I wish that every child, every teen, every person had even one place where they felt so regarded and deeply loved.

If we can find even a fraction of that love in a family, in a team, in a support network, in any kind of group—that is real healing power. That can help us through the darkest of moments. We can survive anything if we truly believe we are not alone. Anything.

Our kids, our teens, our people—they crave real connections. What I can attest to knowing, from both my beloved Refuge family as well as my sweet boxing gym, is that *community is everything*. Here are some other things I have learned along the way:

- You do not have to agree with someone to validate their experiences. It can make a world of difference to say, "I hear that you believe ___, and your feelings about __ matter."
- Be genuinely approachable. If a child can already anticipate a negative reaction (whether factual or not), they are less likely to disclose much of anything.
- If kids have unshakable positive beliefs about themselves, they are more protected than they could ever be.
- When we say, "I was once a kid, too, you know," it can render any further conversation null and void. Different decades, worlds of experiences apart.
- Teens are more likely to have an important conversation when eye contact is not required.
- Educate that the body scale is an unreliable reporter for both weight and worth. Full stop.
- Grief needs space to be held and is not a problem to fix.
- Thoughts that tend toward the negative starting with "What if" can be met with "What if" in the opposite direction, toward health.
- If it is an absolutely honest sentiment, the directive "Help me understand" works well.
- Life simply does not get easier; we get better at our capacity to deal with it.

Closing Thoughts

- We are never going to get it perfectly right, because we are human. But genuinely apologizing when we need to is a game changer.
- Remind our kids that our feelings are never their responsibility. Ever.
- See them for who they are, not who we think they should be.
- Be willing to listen to the potentially mundane in order to pave the way for the potentially crucial conversations.
- Remember that even wanting to love, see, hear, and validate a child is where the real meaning is found; everything else is just bonus material.

NOTES

1. Glennon Doyle, "First the Pain, Then the Rising," *SuperSoul Sessions*, Oprah Winfrey Network, May 10, 2017, 14:44, https://www.youtube.com/watch?v=BpBnGHjda14.
2. Bianca Sparacino, *A Gentle Reminder* (Thought Catalog Books, 2021), 144.
3. Benjamin Zablotsky and Amanda E. Ng, "Mental Health Treatment Among Children Aged 5–17 Years: United States, 2021," NCHS Data Brief No. 472, Hyattsville, MD: National Center for Health Statistics, June 2023, https://dx.doi.org/10.15620/cdc:128144.
4. *Inside Out 2*, written by Meg LeFauve, Dave Holstein, and Kelsey Mann, directed by Kelsey Mann (Pixar Animation Studios, 2024).
5. C.S. Lewis, *The Problem of Pain* (Harper One, 1940), 176.
6. Brené Brown, "Listening to Shame," TED Talk, March 16, 2012, https://www.youtube.com/watch?v=psN1DORYYV0.
7. "Quick—What's That Smell? Mammal Brains Identify Type of Scent Faster Than Once Thought," NYU Langone Health, November 16, 2017, https://nyulangone.org/news/quick-whats-smell-mammal-brains-identify-type-scent-faster-once-thought.
8. Elyse Myers, (@elysemyersofficial), "It Gets SO GOOD, I Promise," Facebook reel, December 9, 2024, https://www.facebook.com/watch/?v=1294242888248210.
9. Lisa Dion, workshop presentation, Six Day Synergetic Play Therapy Intensive, March 9–18, 2018, Play Therapy Institute, Boulder, CO.
10. Anna Gephart, "Opinion: 'Barbie' Was Never Anti-Men, but Was Always Anti-Patriarchy," The Eagle, August 29, 2023, https://www.theeagleonline.com/article/2023/08/opinion-barbie-was-never-anti-men-but-was-always-anti-patriarchy.
11. *Barbie*, written by Greta Gerwig and Noah Baumbach, directed by Greta Gerwig (Warner Bros. Pictures, 2023).
12. Brené Brown, *Daring Greatly: How the Courage to Be Vulnerable Transforms the Way We Live, Love, Parent, and Lead* (Avery, 2012), page 75.
13. Jonathan Haidt, *The Anxious Generation: How the Great Rewiring of Childhood Caused an Epidemic of Mental Illness* (Penguin Press, 2024), 71.
14. John O'Donohue, "The Inner Landscape of Beauty," interview by Krista Tippett, *On Being*, February 28, 2008, https://onbeing.org/programs/john-odonohue-the-inner-landscape-of-beauty/.
15. Brené Brown, "The Power of Vulnerability," TED Talk, January 3, 2011, https://www.youtube.com/watch?v=iCvmsMzlF7o.
16. Mariska Hargitay, "Mariska Hargitay Shares Her Experience in Her Own Words: A Rape. A Reckoning. A Renewal," *People Magazine*, January 10, 2024, https://people.com/mariska-hargitay-experience-rape-renewal-reckoning-8424247.

Notes

[17] "All You Wanna Do," *Six the Musical*, written by Toby Marlow and Lucy Moss, lyrics by Toby Marlow and Lucy Moss, 2017.
[18] Brené Brown, "Listening to Shame," TED Talk, March 2012, https://www.ted.com/talks/brene_brown_listening_to_shame.
[19] Glennon Doyle, "First the Pain, Then the Rising," *Super Soul Sessions*, Oprah Winfrey Network, May 10, 2017, https://www.youtube.com/watch?v=BpBnGHjda14.
[20] "Understanding the Impact of Childhood Grief," JAG Institute, accessed February 25, 2025, https://judishouse.org/childhood-bereavement/impact-2/.
[21] Hope Edelman, *Motherless Daughters: The Legacy of Loss* (Da Capo Lifelong Books, 2006), 23.
[22] Aaron Freeman, "Planning Ahead Can Make a Difference in the End," *All Things Considered*, NPR, June 1, 2005, https://www.npr.org/2005/06/01/4675953/planning-ahead-can-make-a-difference-in-the-end.
[23] Anne Lamott, *Somehow: Thoughts on Love* (Riverhead Books, 2024), 63.
[24] Sandra Levins, *Was It the Chocolate Pudding?: A Story for Little Kids About Divorce*, illustrated by Bryan Langdo (Magination Press, 2005).
[25] Brené Brown, *Daring Greatly: How the Courage to Be Vulnerable Transforms the Way We Live, Love, Parent, and Lead*, Avery, September 11, 2012, 91.
[26] Pema Chodron, *When Things Fall Apart: Heart Advice for Difficult Times* (Shambala Publications, 2016), 71.
[27] Jo Harkin, *Tell Me an Ending* (Scribner, 2022).
[28] Susan Rose Blauner, *How I Stayed Alive When My Brain Was Trying to Kill Me: One Person's Guide to Suicide Prevention* (William Morrow Paperbacks, 2003), 17.
[29] Glennon Doyle, "The Erasing," blog entry, *Momastery: We Can Do Hard Things*, September 30, 2015, https://momastery.com/blog/2015/09/30/the-erasing.
[30] Viktor Frankl, *Man's Search for Meaning* (Beacon Press, 2006), 68.
[31] Stephen Porges, qtd. in Nicole C. Kear, "The Vagus Nerve: Everything Everywhere All at Once," *Oprah Daily*, Feb 21, 2024, https://www.oprahdaily.com/life/health/a46699843/vagus-nerve-what-to-know/.
[32] Glennon Doyle, *Untamed*, The Dial Press, March 10, 2020, Kindle ed., chap. 12.
[33] "A Very Merry Ginny and Georgia Christmas Special," *Ginny and Georgia*, written by Angela Nissel, directed by Danishka Esterhazy, aired January 5, 2023, on Netflix.
[34] "Kimmy Goes Outside!" *The Unbreakable Kimmy Schmidt*, created by Tina Fey and Robert Carlock, pilot episode aired March 6, 2015, on Netflix.
[35] Prentis Hemphill, *What It Takes to Heal: How Transforming Ourselves Can Change The World* (Random House, 2024), xii.
[36] Lisa Dion, "Be Yourself – Therapist Authenticity in the Playroom," Synergetic Play Therapy Institute, accessed February 25, 2025, https://synergeticplaytherapy.com/be-yourself/.

ABOUT THE AUTHOR

STACY SCHAFFER, M.A., is a compassionate and dedicated children's therapist in Arvada, Colorado, with over twenty years of experience helping children navigate emotional and behavioral challenges. Specializing in both grief and Synergetic Play Therapy, Stacy creates a safe and nurturing place where people can take a deep breath. She also leads youth and family programs at The Refuge, a non-profit community center dedicated to healing community. Knowing children, teens, and young adults can feel heard and empowered energizes her soul and helps redeem all that has been lost. Outside therapy, Stacy loves spending quality time with amazing friends, surfing in the summer, reading at any opportunity, loving her golden retriever, Willow, kickboxing year round, and daydreaming about being a stand-up comedian. She continues to do her own therapeutic work in order to be genuine about her passion for healing. She loves to travel, but one can only escape the real world so many times. Her commitment to ensuring that children, teens, and young adults feel heard and empowered drives her practice, which offers essential support and recovery for those in need.

www.ingramcontent.com/pod-product-compliance
Lightning Source LLC
Chambersburg PA
CBHW032224080426
42735CB00008B/698